AT THE INTERFACE:

THEOLOGY AND VIRTUAL REALITY

MARY TIMOTHY PROKES, F.S.E.

FOREWORD BY ARCHBISHOP JOHN P. FOLEY

At the Interface: Theology and Virtual Reality

Published by Fenestra Books™
610 East Delano Street, Suite 104, Tucson, Arizona 85705 U.S.A.
www.fenestrabooks.com

International Standard Book Number: 1-58736-304-6
Library of Congress Control Number: 2004101074

In gratitude to

*The Franciscan Sisters of the Eucharist,
La Verna Center Community,
and
those who press us toward
a more intense interface with Real Presence*

Contents

FOREWORD

In contemporary literature regarding either theology or communications, it is unlikely that it would be possible to find another treatment of "The Theological Implications of Virtual Reality."

The subject, however, is of great importance. Virtual reality is more than just "a sign of the times." For many, virtual reality is their principal world; they live in great measure in a world of virtual relationships.

I would hope that a proper realization of the meaning of "virtual reality" would help some people accept the reality of the truths of faith.

The preface of the Mass at Christmas asks us to be led through the Word made visible to a love of the God we cannot see. In fact, a key belief of our Christian faith is that the Word, the Second Person of the Blessed Trinity, did become flesh and that Jesus Christ is the God-man.

St. Thomas Aquinas says of the fact that Jesus gave us His Body and Blood under the appearances of bread and wine:

> "Sight, touch and taste in Thee are each deceived;
>
> The ear alone most safely is believed."

Sister M. Timothy Prokes, F.S.E., initials which stand for the Franciscan Sister of the Eucharist, has obviously been nourished through reception of and meditation on the Eucharist in her examination of the theological implications of virtual reality.

Having read her entire book, which is relatively brief but also demanding and stimulating, I concur fully in its conclusion:

"The task of theology at the beginning of the Third Millennium is clear: the explication of the profound gifts of the faith, received at ever-greater depth, enriched by interdisciplinary insights, but keenly alert to the most pervasive 'sign of the times'—virtual reality."

Archbishop John P. Foley
President
Pontifical Council for Social Communications
Palazzo San Carlo, Vatican City

INTRODUCTION

Will human nature itself change? Will we soon pass some point where we are so altered by our imaginations and inventions as to be unrecognizable to Shakespeare or the writers of the ancient Greek plays?

No one knows, but many are trying to imagine such a world. They describe our children and grandchildren as no longer being like us. They call them trans-human, or post-human.[1]

What are the central issues for faith and theology in the opening decade of the Third Christian Millennium? Responses to that question may vary, but surely the issues raised by Michael Heim in the above quotation indicate the need for urgent consideration of questions concerning what it means to be human, and what it means to interact with "imagined worlds" in a so-called "trans-human" or "post-human" milieu.

Jesus Christ did not "do theology." Rather, he came as personal fulfillment of Divine Revelation in the flesh. *His*

---

1.   Michael Heim, *The Metaphysics of Virtual Reality* (New York, 1993), p. 111.

1

questions evoked the kind of reflection that would lead to Christian theology. Amid the common events of life, whether he was at table, on journey, or speaking with menders of nets and tax collectors, he penetrated to the truths of persons and situations by asking crucial questions that touched the roots of life, and opened the *meaning* of all that exists. He asked: "What are you looking for?" (Jn. 1:38)[2] "Whose likeness and inscription is this?" (Matt. 22:20) "Did not he who made the outside make the inside also?" (Lk. 11:40) "What man of you, if his son asks him for bread, will give him a stone?" (Mt. 7:9) "If you know how to interpret the look of the sky, can you not read the signs of the times?" (Matt. 16:3) The questions of Jesus Christ are timeless, prodding each generation of believers to ask them anew in the context of their own historical moment.

It is that final question, however, that presently burns with particular intensity: **"Can you not read the signs of the times?"** I suggest that, currently, no "sign of the times" requires greater attention from the Church and contemporary theologians than the rapidly developing complex of life-changing events summarized in the term *Virtual Reality.* Perhaps the most significant theological questions of the present decade derive from one that is very fundamental: **How does "virtual reality" pertain to the divine realities of faith revealed in Jesus Christ?**

Immediately it is necessary to ask: what is *virtual reality*? How much does it already pervade daily life? In previous millennia it was primarily philosophers who grappled with questions concerning the "really real." Today, questions concerning reality take variant forms, such as "How do we dis-

---

2.   Unless they are incorporated in quoted materials, Scriptural passages cited in this book follow the translation of *The Jerusalem Bible,* Alexander Jones, *et al* eds. (Garden City, New York, 1966).

tinguish what is real from what is virtual? How does that which is virtual interface with the real? Does the 'virtual' have a validity that equals or even surpasses the 'real'?" These are questions that currently stir the imagination and the genius of scientists and technicians, probing as deeply as Michael Heim's question: "Will human nature change itself?" The *manner* in which these questions are being *answered* in the secular arena is no longer abstract, since practical applications of "the virtual" are pervasive in medicine and pharmacy, in electronic forms of entertainment, robotic devices, and "smart bombs" that ferret out precise targets.

It is the purpose of this book to address *virtual reality* as a prime sign of our times, to explore its meaning, and to cite basic reasons why it presents urgent issues for Catholic faith and theological study. To turn an ancient phrase: what has Christian Faith to do with Virtual Reality? Being neither a scientist nor a technician, I come to these questions as theologian: one whose faith seeks understanding (and, increasingly, in this privileged moment of history, one *whose faith seeks embodiment*). Theological reflection always takes place within a particular segment of time. It is necessarily immersed in specific cultures, with their interwoven social and political fabric. It is in that context that I propose "virtual reality" in its complex and rapidly developing applications as a major focus for the attention of the Church and Catholic theology in the emergent years of the Third Millennium.

To cite virtual reality as a crucial theological issue at the beginning of the Third Millennium is not to signal a complete rejection of all that the term encompasses. There are benefits accruing from some of its applications. There is need, however, for awareness that increasingly greater immersion in the "virtual" does have profound ramifications concerning the basic truths of Catholic Faith. Immersion in anything involves familiarity. Familiarity, however (especially when it provides convenience and pleasure) can also produce a loss of perspective. It can dull the ability to recognize how the seemingly routine and the ordinary are affected by unsound thought and praxis. Specifically, increased immersion in the "virtually real," together with the convenience and novelty afforded by its applications, can obscure discernment regarding ways in which the "virtual" conditions and changes both experience and understanding of what it means to be authentically human.

From a theological perspective, I suggest that virtual reality impacts not only upon our understanding of Divine Persons, but upon an understanding of creation and what it means to be a human person created in the image and likeness of God. In the following chapters it will be necessary 1) to explore a basic understanding of virtual reality, and its varying levels; and 2) to indicate how "the virtual" impacts upon the way we experience the *realities* of Incarnation, Redemption, sacramental life, freedom, and responsibility. Concomitantly, it is vital to see how aspects of the virtual touch upon such fundamental realities as enduring truth, freedom, and continuity of meaning, as well as presence and absence.

This book is an attempt to address in basic ways the cogent need for theological reflection on the "coincidence of opposites" summed up in the oxymoron "virtual reality." It is not the purpose here to provide ready answers to the immense questions that virtual reality raises. This book can only provide a basis for beginning earnest dialogue, study, and pastoral insight. As such, it simply provides a kind of "theological primer" on a matter of vital concern. That is why it will be necessary in ensuing chapters to describe how the term "virtual reality" is understood, and to show how and why it implicates the most fundamental aspects of Christian faith and life. From the outset, it must be asked to what extent daily life is already noticeably conditioned and changed by "the virtual."

A succinct example demonstrates how immersion in the "virtual" can condition perceptions of what is ordinary, familiar. Recently, on two successive evenings of the Christmas season, guests who entered our convent home and saw logs burning in the fireplace asked spontaneously, "Is that *real* fire?" Since many homes are now equipped with simulated "flaming logs," a *genuine* log-fire in the urban hearth can seem a novelty.

Another indication of contemporary immersion in the "virtual" is the content of newspaper cartoons. In order for something to be considered humorous, there must be a sufficiently *common* understanding of images, situations and terms in order that swift recognition of them poses an incongruity. Recently, a "Mr. Boffo" cartoon bore the tagline: "Another way to tell when you're dealing with someone who hasn't yet got a firm handle on technology." The accompanying sketch portrayed an executive addressing the telephone on his desk: "And how are you today, Mr. Button Box?" A "Frank and Ernest" cartoon dubbed "Shakespeare 1999" had a bemused Hamlet uttering, "To be or not to be...or maybe virtual reality?"

In the United States' capital (Washington, D.C.), photo vendors set up life-size, well-contrived images of the President and the First Lady, offering an opportunity for visitors to "have their picture taken with the First Couple" so that they can take home feigned evidence of an encounter with the president. In fact, the photographic and technical ability to blend, delete, or improvise photographic images has become so sophisticated that photos can no longer provide irrefutable evidence of an actual occurrence. The genuine and the virtual are too easily confused by photographic sleight-of-hand.

How *pervasive*, though, has the virtual become? *The Washington Post*, in a "Millennium Special," October 8, 1999, noted that the amount of data stored on a microchip will double every eighteen months and that the modern home is already "wired to the gills."[3] The special millennial issue of the *Post* described the home of the future as being "proactive." For example, medicine cabinets will remind people to take their pills. It will be unnecessary to "boot up" a computer because the Internet will always be there, like a dial tone, permeating the house:

> In theory, your English muffin will be able to communicate with muffins throughout the nations of the former English Empire...the truly smart house will have no encumbrances, and won't sit around waiting for orders from the boss. You want a refrigerator that not only detects when you're out of milk (and orders another gallon specifying 2 percent milk fat), but one that goes the extra mile and discovers that behind the half-used jar of Ragu, there lurks some rice pilaf that is rapidly and catastrophically degenerating into a bacterial metropolis. You want the fridge to flash that headline on its visual display: Microbial Manhattan Behind Ragu.[4]

Some computers now "address" the owner on a first-name basis as part of the booting-up process. A simulated voice with a gracious, rather comforting tone, conveys the notion that the technical coding within the "desk-top box" knows the user on a first-name basis and offers a personal relationship. "Hello, Norma," a programmed computer

---

3.   Joel Achenbach, "FUTURE Perfect: Your house is about to get very smart. Ready?" *The Washington Post* (October 8, 1999), p. H1ff.
4.   "FUTURE Perfect," p. H16.

greets an owner, as a simulated butterfly flits across the brilliantly-colored computer screen.

Is This a Theological Concern?

How does all of this touch the depths of faith? What theological issues emerge from such familiar and ingenious applications of the virtual? If persons of faith and theological insight have not perceived the ways in which *virtual reality* radically touches the core issues of faith, many who are involved in the study and research of the virtual certainly do. A few titles of books written by those involved in the cybernetic milieu should give pause to theologians: N. Katherine Hayles' *How We Became Posthuman: Virtual Bodies in Cybernetics, Literature, and Information*; Frank Tipler's *The Physics of Immortality: Modern Cosmology, God, and the Resurrection of the Dead*; and Warren Brown, *et al*, editor, *Whatever Happened to the Human Soul?*

In order to open some of the basic questions concerning the impact of *virtual reality* on matters of faith and its understanding, it will be necessary in the ensuing chapters 1) to establish a basis for recognizing theological issues by describing briefly the various levels of *virtual reality* and some predominant ways in which it is understood and expressed; 2) to indicate the manner in which advanced applications of *virtual reality* impinge upon real body-persons, and particularly the reality of the Incarnate Jesus Christ; 3) to reflect on real presence and real absence, showing the implications for Eucharistic faith and the imaging of Trinitarian relationships; 4) to consider how the meaning of the virtual touches upon real freedom; and 5) to ask how the virtual impacts upon the relation of body-persons to supernatural reality. Concerning each of these, it will be crucial to consider how it pertains to Christian faith and theological insight.

Faith is a profound gift. To understand it ever more deeply through reverent probing of its meaning is a privilege. It is understood that this book is only an opening of the question: How significant for Catholic faith and theological reflection is that contemporary sign of the times termed *virtual reality?* It is in that context that this book is offered as a threshold piece, and is not intended as an all-encompassing treatment of the question, nor a comprehensive attempt to respond to its deepest implications. It is more like the tentative song of a bird at dawn, announcing a new day streaked with lightning flashes from an impending storm system that is ripe for both refreshing rain and damaging winds. In order to suggest why virtual reality is a significant matter for theological reflection, it is essential to sketch briefly what is included in that burgeoning cloud of possibilities that already envelops a new day for humanity.

1

WHAT IS VIRTUAL REALITY?

*V**irtual Reality:*** the term is an oxymoron. For centuries the word "virtual" pertained to *potential* beings, while "reality" referred to *existent* beings. Michael Heim writes that dictionary definitions such as *Webster's* identify the *virtual* as "being in essence or effect though not formally recognized or admitted" while *reality* is "a real event, entity, or state of affairs." Now, however, says Heim, "We paste the two together and read: 'Virtual reality is an event or entity that is real in effect but not in fact.'"[1] In other words, there is an *effectiveness without factual existence.*

While he acknowledges that there is no general agreement concerning what *constitutes* virtual reality[2] (even among those working in this area), Heim says that seven divergent concepts can be noted to describe it. It is helpful in beginning this work on theological implications of virtual

---

1. Michael Heim, *The Metaphysics of Virtual Reality* (New York, 1993), p. 111.
2. "Virtual reality" will sometimes be termed *VR* in this book.

reality to name and briefly describe these seven concepts distinguished by Heim in order to reflect on *both* the positive and the problematic aspects of virtual reality which they represent. Heim distinguishes seven levels of *VR*:

- Simulation
- Interaction
- Artificiality
- Immersion
- Telepresence
- Full-body immersion
- Networked communication

While technological applications of the virtual among these categories escalate daily, the seven-stage progression described by Heim already in 1993 remains useful as an introductory framework. It is important to sketch briefly what these concepts mean.

Simulation, the initial concept, means the *seeming degree of realism* that sharp visual and audio images evoke. Heim gives the example of computer graphics, and of landscapes produced on the GE Aerospace "visionics" equipment. They are so photorealistic that they offer "real-time texture-mapped worlds through which users can navigate."[3] This technology which is employed in military flight simulators is also applied in the fields of medicine, education, and entertainment. The "as if" quality of sophisticated simulators can be of considerable advantage for training purposes. Pilots, for example, within the confines of a flight simulator can practice take-offs and landings in safety while saving resources and gaining expertise.

---

3.   Michael Heim, *The Metaphysics of Virtual Reality*, p. 113.

Interaction is a second level of *VR*. For some, says Heim, virtual reality means "any electronic representation with which they can interact."[4] For example, even though it is not a "desktop," a computer is treated *as if it were* because the icons make it seem that there are actual "files" in the diminutive workings of the computer and that we can drag them, like cardboard folders, to metal trash cans when we want to clear the desktop. Although there is no actual paper, or cardboard files or trash cans, *interaction with the virtual images makes them seem real* in the process of working out a project. Outside of this interaction with a computer program, the diminutive "trash can" would routinely be considered virtual-only, but in working out a project they serve handily in miniature electronic transactions that would, in the past, require real paper and metal, weight, and muscular dexterity. In this "interaction" level of VR, Heim includes "virtual persons" known through telephone or computer networks (including politicians and entertainers), and "virtual places" such as virtual universities, where online classes are attended in virtual classrooms and students "socialize in virtual cafeterias."[5]

Artificiality is a third concept of virtual reality. Currently, our environment is so thoroughly "wired," so smothered in asphalt and concrete and otherwise reconstructed that a significant portion of the planet can already be termed an artifice. Consumers have become so habituated to the artificial that a straight-faced home furnishing salesman can hawk a piece of furniture as "genuine simulated walnut." Artificial flowers can so closely resemble their organic counterpart that many persons prefer them: the artificial blooms are maintenance-free and retain the look of freshness. In fact, splendid

---

4.   Michael Heim, *The Metaphysics of Virtual Reality*, p. 113.
5.   Michael Heim, *The Metaphysics of Virtual Reality*, p. 114.

natural blossoms often evoke the comment that "they are so beautiful they look artificial."

Immersion: This understanding of virtual reality involves the use of specific hardware and software combinations, employed with ever greater technological sophistication. Initial phases of immersion-*VR* featured the use of stereoscopic three-dimensional displays, supported by a head-tracking device, a data-glove and hand-held devices to add feedback. In this view of virtual reality, the object is to attain "sensory immersion in a virtual environment" says Heim. The purpose in using the head-mounted displays is to cut off visual and audio sensation from the *real* world outside in order to replace them with *computer-generated sensations.*[6] Simulation and sensation are combined. Flight simulators, for example, employ feedback that may connect with an actual aircraft. Pilots, either in their training or in upgrading their licenses, feel immersed, fully present in a virtual world that is connected to the real world. Immersion-*VR* is more specific than the general category of artificiality.

Telepresence is *robotic* presence. This is a crucial concept of *VR.* Heim writes, "To be present somewhere yet present there remotely is to be there virtually!"[7] In the application of this kind of technology, a significant boundary is crossed: in robotic telepresence, there is real-time effectiveness in a real-world location without a human person in the flesh being present at that location. For example, in "telepresence medicine" a doctor can work inside a patient's body without being bodily present at the location. It is a kind of double-edged sword, writes Heim:

---

6.   Cf. Michael Heim, *The Metaphysics of Virtual Reality*, p. 115.
7.   Michael Heim, *The Metaphysics of Virtual Reality*, p. 116.

By permitting immersion, telepresence offers the operator a great control over remote processes. But at the same time, a psycho-technological gap opens up between doctor and patient. Surgeons complain of losing hands-on contact as the patient evaporates into a phantom of bits and bytes.[8]

This highly-developed employment of immersion-*VR* can become still more complex, in what can be described as full-body immersion.

Full-body Immersion. There are no head-displays or gloves here. Myron Krueger, who is sometimes termed the "father of virtual reality," utilizes equipment that *projects a user's body in a manner that enables it to interact with graphic images and objects on a screen.* Now, in ordinary daily life, there is obviously some interaction between a person who is observing another person or object, and the object of their sight. But something much more radical is meant here. As Heim points out, *the burden of input rests with the computer,* which "reads" the body's free movements. In this form of *VR*, cameras follow a user's body and synthesize its movements with an artificial environment.

Networked Communications. More is intended by this term than the familiar use of the Internet. In this seventh view of *VR*, says Heim, there is reference to a *new communications medium.* He uses as example the RB2 or "Reality Built for Two" System which connects virtual worlds. Jaron Lanier refers to this as "post-symbolic communication." It can involve communication "beyond verbal or body language to take on magical, alchemical properties."[9]

---

8.   Michael Heim, *The Metaphysics of Virtual Reality,* p. 117.
9.   Michael Heim, *The Metaphysics of Virtual Reality,* p. 118.

It must be underscored that Heim's book bears a 1993 copyright! Incremental developments in cyberspace technology make the above summation of seven concepts of virtual reality seem very elemental. Nevertheless, they are foundational, and current developments stem from them. The purpose here is to discuss their impact on faith and theological endeavors.

Theology is faith seeking understanding. For a Catholic theologian, it consists of dedicated scholarly research and reflection on Revelation as conveyed in Scripture and Sacred Tradition, in union with the Magisterium.[10] The Gospels describe how Jesus Christ, the personal *complete realization* of divine Revelation, laid the foundations for those seeking an authentic understanding of faith. Above all, in His Last Discourse, He said that faith involves a waiting upon and a receptivity for the Holy Spirit—the divine personal indweller—who "will lead you to the complete truth...and he will tell you of the things to come." (Jn. 16:13) The context of Jesus' personal revelation was relationships, divine and human. He consistently showed how intimately faith touched the concrete realities of daily life in the body. To open his listeners to the meaning of creation, life, and the Kingdom, he often asked questions relating the most profound truths to the simplest of material things and events— such as bread, fish, salt, nets and the payment of taxes. He showed that the elements of daily life have a potential exceeding ordinary expectations.

To an obtuse crowd bent on testing Him, and asking Him to show them a sign from heaven, Jesus replied: "In the

---

10.   Cf. *Dei Verbum*, the Second Vatican Council's Dogmatic Constitution of Revelation, in *Vatican Council II: The Conciliar and Post Conciliar Documents*, new revised ed., Austin Flannery gen. ed. (Grand Rapids, MI, 1992), pp. 750-765.

evening you say, 'It will be fine; there is a red sky,' and in the morning, 'Stormy weather today; the sky is red and overcast.' You know how to read the face of the sky but you cannot read the signs of the times.'" (Matt. 16:3) Redness of sky was no threat in itself: knowing how to "read it" correctly was the issue, so that appropriate responses could be made. The ensuing chapters of this book will attempt to read the significance of virtual reality as a cogent sign of the times within the context of faith seeking understanding.

2

VIRTUAL REALITY AND REAL BODY-PERSON

Our whole existence is the acceptance or rejection of
the mystery which we are, as we find our poverty referred
to the mystery of the fullness. The pre-existent object of
our acceptance or refusal, of the decision which is the
deed of our life, is the mystery which we are. And this
mystery is our nature, because the transcendence which
we are and which we accomplish brings our existence and
God's existence together: and both as mystery.[1]

"*O*ur whole existence is the acceptance or rejection
of the mystery which we are," says Karl Rahner.
To see why "the virtual" presents issues of
extreme importance for theological investigation, it is crucial
to begin by asking: what is the reality, meaning, and destiny
of the living body-person? Christian faith affirms the
astounding truth that human body-persons are created in the

---

1.   Karl Rahner, "On the Theology of the Incarnation," in *Theological Investigations IV,* trans. Kevin Smyth (Baltimore, 1966), p.
108.

17

image and likeness of God and destined for eternal communion with God. That implies several fundamental assertions: 1) that *created* persons are divinely willed for their own sake and are not simply the product of human invention[2]; 2) that to be human is to bear a divine image and likeness; and 3) that the mystery of divine-human relationship is an enduring reality. As Karl Rahner emphasized, the human person is a mystery. He further clarified that mystery is not to be confused with the "still undisclosed unknown." Rather, mystery is "the impenetrable which is already present and does not need to be fetched...therefore not something provisional which is one day to be done away with or which could in fact be non-mysterious. It is the propriety which always and necessarily characterizes God—and through him, us."[3] Both theological reflection on faith, and the reading of that "sign of the times" called virtual reality, participate in the meaning of mystery. Since this book necessarily involves consideration of human embodiment, it is essential to note that whenever terms such as *body-person, the living body,* and *lived body* are used in this work, they refer to the *whole person* as an embodied presence in the world.

Within the marvelous complexity of a body-person, created in the divine image and likeness, there is an astounding array of capacities which express the unique mystery of each person. To touch any one facet of the person is to touch the whole lived body, which divine revelation manifests is destined for eternal life. Prior to the final decades of the twentieth century, it was commonly held within Western

---

2.   See *Gaudium et spes*, Pastoral Constitution on the Church in the Modern World, #24, in *Vatican Council II: The Conciliar and Post Conciliar Documents*, Austin Flannery gen. ed. (New York, 1992), p. 925.

3.   Karl Rahner, "On the Theology of the Incarnation," p. 108.

Civilization that *human persons* were distinct from vegetable and animal levels of life as well as from technological and mechanical devices. Surely there were literary works that developed fantasy figures such as Jekyll and Hyde, Superman, and frenzied scientists bent on fashioning mechanical monsters. Such imaginative characters have fascinated readers and theater audiences over a long period of time. Gradually, however, some distinctions between the human and other entities have become muted as well as disputed. In recent research and experimentation, there is the fashioning of hybrid entities, combining specific human, animal, vegetable and technical components. The boundaries of the human have been severely questioned by some members of scientific, technical and ethical disciplines. It can no longer be presumed that there is a commonly held understanding of the "human" or what constitutes an integral boundary between the human person and other organic or technical beings. This is matter for serious theological concern since it implicates an understanding of divine and human persons—indeed, it touches every aspect of Christian faith.

While it is impossible, within the purpose of this work, to explore the totality of ways in which the boundary of the human is being questioned, there must be recognition of dominant ways in which advanced applications of virtual reality already trespass the boundaries of what it means to be human.

Immediately, in order to explore these implications, some distinctions must be made concerning "the virtual" and its applied use, and the human gifts of imagination and creativity. As will be evident throughout this book, it is not the "the virtual" as a basic human experience that is questioned here, but its applications in ways that distort or replace the human. Indeed, there are technical applications of the virtual which assist in the disclosure of some *realities* that exceed human intellectual measurement, but which are awaiting discovery. For example, extraordinary insights into the micro and macro aspects of the universe are gifts, attained through the work of dedicated scientists and technologists as an essential task for humanity at this historical juncture.

The Human Genome Project has documented the sequence of the human genome (the organism's complete set of DNA). The "DNA sequence" is the term used to describe the side-by-side arrangement of "bases" along a strand of DNA. The human genome is constituted by some 3 billion of these "base pairs." Yet, the billions of pairs in this sequence are composed of *variations* on only four nitrogen-containing "bases": adenine (A), thymine (T), cytosine (C), and guanine (G). The recorded findings of the Human Genome Project are equivalent to a multiple-volume set of encyclopedias. Every cell of the human body, with the exception of mature red blood cells, contains a complete genome, and its order "spells out the exact instructions required to create a particular organism with its own unique traits."[4] While intimately related to the entire human patterning, the intricate design of *each* person's DNA is uniquely expressed in bone and eye and heart. Note that the DNA of all organisms is composed of these same four chemical, physical components. The findings concerning DNA show a marvelous relatedness among the non-personal works of creation and that which is the distinctly human sequence.

In complement to this marvelous *micro* documentation concerning the patterning of the living human body, there is a growing corpus of scientific and technical knowledge and imagery concerning the *macro* scale of the universe. The recently refurbished Hubble Telescope has been relaying

---

4.   Media Guide to the Human Genome Project, (accessed) http://www.ornl.gov/hgmis/resource/media.html, p. 4.

photos of events "happening" billions of years ago, at distances which befuddle thought. Both micro and macro findings call upon the human imagination to receive their implications. In terms of "size," as unique gift of God's creation, *the human body-person is like a centering-point of the macro-micro universe.* It throbs with activity and freshness, composed physically of that which is infinitesimally small, yet in interdependence with that which is incomprehensibly vast. In each case, the beings which exist within the mystery of divine largesse are not the products of human ingenuity, but the realities of divine creation available to human recognition and given for responsible human dominion. In order to see what such cosmological items have to do with the virtual, it is also necessary and helpful to acknowledge and appreciate the gift of human imagination.

Among the interior faculties of a human person are memory and imagination, those abilities which enable remembrance of what has been experienced (persons, non-personal beings, and events) and then the capacity to re-fashion them creatively. It is through the use of imagination that we are able to scan the blurs of light on photos relayed from the Hubble telescope and make statements such as, "The farther out we look, the farther back in time we see. Light takes 50 million years to arrive from M87, so we see it as it appeared 50 million years ago."[5]

In formulating such statements, it is the human imagination that allows analogies to be made, showing relationships unattainable through ordinary use of the senses (and thus not *directly* attainable by the intellect). Contemporary scientific instruments give evidence of entities which are either prodigiously small or inconceivably immense, at distances,

---

5.   Kathy Sawyer, "Unveiling the Universe," *National Geographic* (October, 1999), p. 30.

temperatures, and speeds beyond our ken. Through the imaginative use of simple words and images to enfold what surpasses our grasp, "the virtual" is helpful, linking the familiar with the staggeringly "other." Sawyer writes, for example: "Big bang theory holds that everything in the known universe—all time, space, energy, and matter—was once contained in a point of infinite density known as a singularity. Scientists leave the 'why' of that state of affairs to priests and poets. But in the next instant, they theorize, this point began expanding madly in size—pinhead, grapefruit, basketball—to a radius expressed in incomprehensibly large numbers."[6] In her comparison, Sawyer uses metaphorical language—linking what is familiar to that which is beyond ordinary experience. In such instances, it is the "the virtual" that supports the human memory and imagination in the process of intellective understanding.

IMAGINATION AND THE VIRTUAL

The human imagination, then, is an encounter point with virtual reality, as described in its various aspects by Michael Heim. It must be reiterated that imagination is one of the fundamental gifts of the human person. Long before the Hubble telescope mapped distant galaxies, shepherds and astrologers scanned the night sky and associated configurations of stars and planets with realities close at hand such as dippers, bears, and a hunter with a sword on his belt.

How imagination and memory are nourished or wounded in childhood (in and through the body) has life-long significance. Surrounded by adults who may be preparing meals, carrying out business transactions, or discussing

---

6.   Kathy Sawyer, "Unveiling the Universe," p. 20.

politics, children freely converse with imaginary playmates and play in fantasy worlds of their own inner construction *within the real, person-inhabited world that surrounds them*. If genuine danger threatens them, children will either abandon their imaginary environs and seek safety with real persons in an actual world, or resort to severance from what is real, in order to seek refuge from what is threatening. The interior vividness of a child's imagination, coupled with memory, is the splendid forerunner of adult poetry, of artistic and technical invention. With the maturing gift of imagination comes the capacity to meditate, to form analogies, to savor that which is beautiful, and to envision the possibilities of scientific and technological invention. All of these find their basis in the bodily senses which convey images and evoke human emotional responses in the intellect, memory and imagination.

Today the gift of imagination, *the encounter point between the real and the virtual*, is being subverted, not only for children, but for persons of all ages. Rapidly-shifting animated figures on television screens and computer monitors frequently distort the appearance of the human body, and portray violence without consequences. Absurd imitations of human and animal figures entice curiosity, but they can also evoke sentimental identification with them, and sometimes foster a supposed "need" for commercial products associated with them. In the early, highly impressionable years of childhood, a plethora of virtual screen characters flood the senses with artificial, simulated understandings of what it means to be the "ideal" human person.[7]

Imperceptibly, from childhood on, viewers of electronic media are induced repeatedly to consider the living body-person *in its reality as a **liability**, a defective instrument that betrays what should constitute the desirable body. The body is portrayed as needing a multitude of enhancements through products and services which are "fortunately" available for the*

right price. Numerous advertisements instill the idea that
viewers need a ready-at-hand arsenal of pharmaceutical and
dietary interventions in order to survive daily life and attain
self-fulfillment. There are artificial wares to alleviate artificially created "needs." Some advertisements assure that the
swallowing of a few capsules will guarantee sexual intimacy.
Others assure glamorous appeal through the ingestion of
food supplements or through cosmetic surgery that will re-
fashion the body according to specification. It is evident that
artificiality and simulation, two elemental levels of virtual
reality, are deeply influencing Western culture at this time in
ways that re-interpret the meaning of the human body. The
promises extend beyond the lived body to products such as
clothing and cars which are described as "sexy" in their own
right and take on personal traits. An advertisement for a car
assured that "A Volvo can save your soul."

Why should this be of particular concern for theological
reflection? Understanding of the lived body is crucial, touching every aspect of a faith-based life. The lifestyle of a
mother already influences the child that she carries in her
womb, and the perceptions and attitudes that she conveys
concerning the lived body will pervade the life of her child.

---

7.   This is not to denounce all imaginative and fanciful illustrated
      productions which have a special appeal for children. When done
      well, such works foster, rather than replace, a child's imagination,
      and through creative *genres* convey truths about human life that
      have enduring meaning. For example, Walt Disney's *Bunny Book*
      (Racine, Wisconsin, 1972) is currently available. It is the repro-
      duction of a 1951 classic children's book. Dr. Seuss, *Oh, the
      Places You'll Go!* (New York, 1990), in playful illustration and
      humorous verse, deals with the "Great Balancing Act" of life
      itself, as the dust jacket notes. It can be termed a "brief gradua-
      tion speech" for both nursery school grads and medical school
      achievers because it articulates a truth about life's challenges.

In turn, adults must grapple with the ingrained images and habits that influenced them from their childhood.

In his book *Unless You Become Like This Child,* Hans Urs von Balthasar probed the saying of Jesus: "Amen I say to you: whoever does not receive the Kingdom of God like a child will not enter into it." (Mk. 10:15) Jesus is "the archetypical child," says von Balthasar, and he never outgrows the profound relationship with the Father, in the Holy Spirit. Moreover, who welcomes the Eternal Son is "not welcoming me but him who sent me." (Mk. 9:27) The context of Jesus' teaching regarding children concerns human identity itself:

> Neither father nor mother would pretend that their contribution has given the child its spirit, its freedom, its immediacy with God.... I speak of the "identity" between the child, an existing and developing reality, and the idea that God has of him, the intention therefore that God wishes to realize with him. This idea and intention is God himself and yet not, in so far as it has the creature for an object. It is precisely on the basis of this even more fundamental "archetypical identity" that we can demonstrate what is specifically Christian in the new, post-Classical manner of evaluating childhood: in Christ, for the first time, we see that in God himself there exists—within his inseparable unity—the distinction between the Father who gives and the Gift which is given (the Son), but only in the unity of the Holy Spirit.... The "archetypical identity," which we discover in creatures within a clear separation of persons who are held together by love, is a creaturely *imago trinitatis,* veiled and yet not wholly invisible.[8]

---

8.   Hans Urs von Balthasar, *Unless You Become Like This Child,*
       trans. Erasmo Leiva-Merikakis (San Francisco, 1991), pp. 16, 17,
       19.

The notion of *what it means to be a human person*, then, is instilled in a child's being from earliest experiences. "The love between a thou and an I inaugurates the reality of a world which is deeper than simple being because of its absolute boundlessness and plenitude,"[9] says von Balthasar. This begins with the intimate relationship between mother and child. All of the attributes associated with children are modeled on that initial two-in-one relationship, that image of Trinitarian relationships that is eminently expressed in the body-persons of mother and child. Whatever is not authentic in their interchanges will have enduring impact, as will pervasive, distorted impressions of what it means to be a human person. One of Jesus' sharpest descriptions of evil concerns the scandalizing of children: "But anyone who is an obstacle to bring down one of these little ones who have faith in me would be better drowned in the depths of the sea with a great millstone round his neck." (Matt. 18:6) This has keen relevance for the connection between the human gift of imagination and the fabrication of virtual bodies, personas and "worlds."

Marie-Laure Ryan comments on the virtual, interactive "genealogy of genres" spawned from the1970's to the present, ranging from "Dungeons and Dragons" to so-called MOO's or "multi-user domains, object-oriented."[10] She terms MOO's the apogee of creative make-believe, combining immersion and interactivity through role-playing in a fictional world. A user creates a MOO persona, describing

---

9.   Hans Urs von Balthasar, *Unless You Become Like This Child*, pp. 17-18.
10.   Marie-Laure Ryan, *Narrative as Virtual Reality: Immersion and Interactivity in Literature and Electronic Media* (Baltimore, 2001), p. 310.

the character's body, personality characteristics, living space and occupation. Ryan writes:

> Once a make-believe identity is established, the user enters the virtual body of his character and plays its role from the inside. He encounters other users playing other characters, and they engage in a dialogue in real time. Most contributions are speech acts (*x* says), but the system also allows the performance of physical actions and even the building of virtual objects...and sometimes comes very close to goal-oriented dramatic action, such as flirting, spying, building castles, telling stories, engaging in love affairs, breaking up, and starting new relationships.... Sherry Turkle reports several cases of MOO users who regard their MOO identities as "more real" than their ROL (rest-of-life) selves.[11]

CONTEMPORARY NEO-DOCETISM

While the simulated and the artificial pervade contemporary understandings of what it means to be embodied in the world, the attempt to *escape* bodily realities has not originated in the present age. Radical separation of matter and "spirit" and the demeaning of body have recurred through past millennia. In early Christianity, *Gnosticism* in variant forms persuaded many that the God of the Old Testament, either out of evil intent or ignorance, had created the present material world and its miseries. Liberation from the body was the ideal set before its followers. In the second century, Tertullian, in his *De Carne Christi,* vigorously addressed a certain Marcion who rejected Christ's birth. Tertullian

---

11.   Marie-Laure Ryan, *Narrative as Virtual Reality,* pp. 311-312.

reminded Marcion that although he scorned human birth, Marcion himself had life by means of it.[12]

Manichaeism, another form of gnosticism which flourished from the third century, convinced even St. Augustine of its arguments for a time. In the Middle Ages, renewed struggles with bodily realities took the form of *Catharism,* or *Albigensianism,* and had great appeal in southern Europe. Similar dualistic movements have recurred through the centuries, sometimes mimicking authentic faith, although the Scriptural presentation of creation affirms the goodness of embodied human persons created male and female in the image and likeness of God.

The present recurrence of difficulties with true embodiment, however, may aptly be termed ***Neo-Docetism.*** In order to see how this relates to various levels of the *virtual,* it is helpful to juxtapose 1) the docetism of early Christian centuries; 2) the reality of Jesus Christ's embodiedness; and 3) current attempts to circumvent bodily realities.

The term "Docetism" derives from the Greek *doceo,* meaning "to seem," and describes a movement that was already countered in some New Testament writings. Since they deemed the body unworthy, Docetists could not affirm that Jesus Christ actually suffered, was crucified and died bodily. He only *seemed* to do this, said the Docetists, because they were convinced that the "Real Jesus" would have

---

12.   Tertullian addresses Marcion in *De Carne Christi,* 4: "You shudder at the child expelled together with its afterbirth and covered with it. You reject the fact that it is straightened with cloths, shaped with oils, laughed at with caresses. Marcion, you spit upon this high respect for nature—then, how were you born? You have hated man during his birth. Then how do you love anybody? ... Surely Christ loved that man, coagulated in uncleanness in the womb, that one brought forth through shameful bodily organs, that one nourished through objects of derision."

escaped such bodily indignities. J. N. D. Kelly summarizes key elements of Docetism in his work *Early Christian Doctrines*:

> Known as Docetism, the distinctive thesis which gave it its name...was that Christ's manhood, and hence His sufferings, were unreal, phantasmal. Clearly its ultimate roots were Graeco-Oriental assumptions about divine impassibility and the inherent impurity of matter.... Docetism was not a simple heresy on its own; it was an attitude which infected a number of heresies, particularly Marcionism and Gnosticism. This attitude is crystallized in a remark of Justin's... "there are some who declare that Jesus Christ did not come in the flesh but only as spirit, and exhibited an appearance...of flesh." Traces of teaching like this are visible in the New Testament itself, and very early in the second century we find Ignatius protesting against "godless people" who claimed that Christ had suffered in appearance only.[13]

Kelly explains that those of Gnostic persuasion thought that Jesus Christ was a compound of two distinct substances in loose liaison: a heavenly Christ, and Jesus as "Son of the Demiurge." Gnostic Christology "was also docetic, either as teaching that the heavenly Christ was invisible, impalpable, or as implying that the lower Christ himself, with whom the heavenly Christ joined Himself, was not real flesh and blood."[14] Among the early Fathers of the Church who countered Docetism were Ignatius of Antioch and Irenaeus. For example, on his way to martyrdom in Rome, Ignatius wrote

---

13.   J. N. D. Kelly, *Early Christian Doctrines* (New York, 1978), p. 141.
14.   J. N. D. Kelly, *Early Christian Doctrines*, p. 142.

to the Smyrnaeans (6, 2) that the Eucharist *is* Christ's flesh, which suffered for us and was raised by the Father.

Repeatedly in the writings of the New Testament there is an emphasis on the reality of Jesus' embodiment both in the circumstances of daily life and in resurrected life. It is a recurring hallmark of John's Gospel, from the Prologue in which John wrote that "The Word was made flesh, he lived among us, and we saw his glory," (Jn. 1:14) to the post-resurrection invitation to Thomas, "Put your finger here; look, here are my hands. Give me your hand; put it into my side. Doubt no longer but believe." (Jn. 20:27)

It is particularly in the sixth chapter of his Gospel that John emphasized the reality of Jesus' embodiment. On the day following the miraculous feeding of the multitude and the night crossing of the lake, Jesus tells those that have sought Him that they have come because "you had all the bread you wanted to eat." (Jn. 6:27) He assures them that while their ancestors were fed manna in the desert, the real food he wants to give them is himself, the bread of life, and this bread "is my flesh for the life of the world." (Jn. 6:51)

> I tell you most solemnly,
> if you do not eat the flesh of the Son of Man
> and drink his blood,
> you will not have life in you.
> Anyone who does eat my flesh and drink my blood
> has eternal life,
> and I shall raise him up on the last day.
> For my flesh is real food
> and my blood is real drink.
> He who eats my flesh and drinks my blood
> lives in me
> and I live in him. (Jn. 6:53-56)

Accepting or rejecting the *reality* of this self-gift promised by Jesus was decisive. It was a "watershed moment," and

John's Gospel relates that the majority of the disciples left Jesus at this point. Turning to the Twelve in His immediate company, Jesus asked if they also chose to leave. Peter responded by asking rhetorically: what alternative could there be, since Jesus had the words of eternal life. In the First Epistle of John there is an emphatic affirmation of the enduring reality of Jesus Christ's body. What has existed from the beginning, writes John, that "we" have heard and seen with our own eyes, touched with our hands: this is the Jesus Christ of whom we speak. "What we have seen and heard we are telling you so that you too may be in union with us." (I Jn. 1:3)

Each of the Gospels witnesses to the reality of Jesus' bodily life, suffering, death and resurrection. In the opening portion of Mark's Gospel there is a description of Jesus' hunger after forty days of fasting in the desert. He travels, is confronted bodily by his adversaries, and is anointed while at table in the house of Simon. The Passion accounts stress the intensity of bodily indignities wrought on Jesus' body: bloody scourging, crowning with thorns, the need for assistance in bearing the cross, and thirst in the final agony. It was not a phantasm that sweated blood in Gethsemane and who was mocked upon being immobilized on the cross.

On the other hand, our present time knows a new, technologically astute kind of Docetism, or *seeming* embodiment. How might the present capacity to re-make human bodiliness and to obviate the limitations of embodiment be named? "Neo-Docetism" or "Bodily Virtualism"? Beyond current estimation that the natural, given body is defective, some fabricators with technological acumen envision ways of re-fashioning those human bodies that are considered unworthy and/or are perceived as having unnecessary liabilities. Besides analyzing the human genome and locating genes responsible for specific diseases, some researchers work at obviating specific genetic traits which parents or researchers deem undesirable. This has spawned a variety of experimental and commercial ventures that already result in the culling of embryos before implantation in the womb, in experimentation on embryonic life, in the selective alteration of genetic patterns, and attempts to clone human life.[15]

In an environment flooded with information and images of hyper-dramatic intensity, it is possible to under-estimate the rapidity with which fundamental societal mores are changing. Many attitudes and practices that have become ordinary, or are even considered "human rights" in the opening years of the Third Millennium, would have been rejected (or considered unthinkable) among people in Western cultures in the mid-twentieth century. It may prove helpful to cite specific examples of such changes. Could anyone have suggested even sixty years ago that their children might be conceived in petri dishes, utilizing donor eggs and carefully selected sperm?

In November 2000, Yang Huanming, Director of the Human Genome Research Center of the Institute of Genetics of the Chinese Academy of Sciences was queried concerning genetic possibilities. When asked if it might be technically possible to "make people into 'invulnerable robot police,' astronauts who don't need to breathe oxygen, sensors

---

15.   See, for example, a sympathetic media report on cloning as response to a human "need to have" a child: Rick Weiss, "Free To Be Me: Would-Be Cloners Pushing the Debate," in *The Washington Post* (May 12, 2002), p. A1. A woman at age 41, suffering from infertility, wants a child, says the report: "'I'm not crazy,' says Catalan, whose ovaries went into premature failure years ago. 'I just want to have a child of my own.' Not a child made from a donor egg provided by someone she doesn't know. Not one adopted from halfway around the globe. She wants a baby genetically related to her. And if that means one who's genetically identified, then so be it."

who can predict earthquakes or 'slaves' who don't eat and only work," researcher Huanming said that it would be possible technically, but scientists have the "job" of preventing scientific achievement from "taking us that far."[16]

A writer in *The Hastings Center Report* observed that "The possibility exists that the increasingly common replacement of body parts with mechanical items will lead eventually to the creation of cybernetic organisms—beings that intimately mix man and machine."[17] In a very condensed period of time, serious discussion moved from the conception of children in petri dishes, to the conceiving of embryos for research and then subsequently killing them, to selling of organs from executed criminals or from living persons seeking money to alleviate their poverty.[18] Disregarding objections from religious leaders, Britain's House of Lords approved the cloning of human embryos in January of 2001.

While it might not appear obvious that these examples are related to the levels of "virtual reality" as described above, there is a keen relationship between such objectification of the human body and employment of the virtual, as noted by

---

16.   "Genetics: Where Do We Draw the Line?" in *World Press Review* (November, 2000), p. 41. It was significant that Huanming spoke of "the mystery of nature." When asked if he would approve of changing people's behavior through genes (for example, experimenting with the "faithful gene" strategy used in making a philandering mouse "faithful") he replied: "If there were a 'faithful gene,' I would rather have it removed from my girlfriend; I would want her to be with me only if she, of her own free will, chose to love me and me only. I would not want her to be loyal to me just because of that gene."

17.   See G. Q. Mcguire, Jr. and Ellen M. McGee, "Implantable Brain Chips? Time for Debate," in *The Hastings Center Report* (January-February, 1999), p. 7.

18.   Cf. "Poor Chinese Selling Their Body Parts, Report Says," (Hong Kong, October 30, 2000) ZENIT.org.

N. Katherine Hayles in *How We Became Posthuman: Virtual Bodies in Cybernetics, Literature, and Information*. She asks:

> What is the posthuman? Think of it as a point of view characterized by the following assumptions. (I do not mean this list to be exclusive or definitive. Rather it names elements found at a variety of sites. It is meant to be suggestive rather than prescriptive.) First, the posthuman view privileges informational pattern over material instantiation, so that embodiment in a biological substrate is seen as an accident of history rather than an inevitability of life. Second, the posthuman considers consciousness, regarded as the seat of human identity in the Western tradition long before Descartes thought he was a mind thinking, as an epiphenomenon, as an evolutionary upstart trying to claim that it is the whole show when in actuality it is only a minor sideshow. Third, the posthuman view thinks of the body as the original prosthesis we all learn to manipulate, so that extending or replacing the body with other prostheses becomes a continuation of a process that began before we were born. Fourth, and most important, by these and other means, the posthuman view configures human being so that it can be seamlessly articulated with intelligent machines. In the posthuman, there are no essential differences or absolute demarcations between bodily existence and computer simulation, cybernetic mechanism and biological organism, robot teleology and human goals.[19]

What is astounding is the rapidity with which these developments have taken place and the casualness with which they are treated. In the opening chapter of her book,

---

19.   N. Katherine Hayles, *How We Became Posthuman: Virtual Bodies in Cybernetics, Literature and Informatics* (Chicago, 1999), pp. 2-3.

Hayles cites a number of ways in which the separation of mind from real body is both envisioned and made attractive. She refers to *Star Trek,* which has an ongoing appeal for both children and adults. Already in the 1950's Norbert Wiener was proposing that, theoretically, it would be possible "to telegraph a human being.... The producers of *Star Trek* operate from similar premises when they imagine that the body can be dematerialized into an informational pattern and rematerialized, without change, at a remote location.... In fact a defining characteristic of the present cultural moment is the belief that information can circulate unchanged among different material substrates. It is not for nothing that 'Beam me up, Scotty,' has become a cultural icon for the global informational society."[20]

The second half of the twentieth century was ripe for a variety of Docetic tendencies since it provided numerous ways of seeing how "improvements" might be made upon defective aspects of the lived body. Consideration of the posthuman view of body as an "original prosthesis" opens the possibility of the real body's replacement with a variety of other prostheses, and brings a sharper realization of the need for awareness of the manner in which the virtual has come to permeate the understanding of the lived body in Western society. The body is perceived to be divisible, replaceable, open to refabrication—even to rematerialization at a distant location.

In such scenarios, the more elemental levels of the virtual are surpassed, and bodily immersion in an artificially constructed world is surpassed by the living body itself being directly restructured in the real world, sometimes redirected/influenced through artificial promptings from without.

---

20.   N. Katherine Hayles, *How We Became Posthuman: Virtual Bodies in Cybernetics, Literature, and Informatics,* pp. 1-2.

Implants and impulses are used to control aspects of the person.[21] In a culture that perceives the human as an assembly of parts that can be improved by outside interventions, it is not surprising that the body itself is treated as a commercial product. Baby body-parts from aborted children are openly packaged and sold, advertised as "fresh" in order to appeal for orders from researchers. Euphemisms can dull perception of realities. It is common to speak of "harvesting" human organs from the dead. It has been suggested recently that a newly-deceased person's body should routinely be considered open to such harvesting of organs, *unless there had been prior express written documentation that the person refused such a disposition of their body.*

VIRTUAL PERSONS

N. Katherine Hayles writes of Macy Conferences on Cybernetics (held from 1943 to 1954), which were instrumental in forging a new paradigm for perceiving human beings. "Henceforth, humans were to be seen primarily as information-processing entities who are *essentially* similar to intelligent machines."[22] She relates how, on reading Hans Moravec's *Mind Children: The Future of Robot and Human Intelligence,* she was horrified to see the author argue that mind could be separated from body. She asks how anyone could think that consciousness could be conveyed to another medium other than the body and remain unchanged. The idea of refashioning the human has become pedestrian, however. A research project posted on the Internet told of using

---

21. See, for example, "An Impulse to Happiness" in *The Washington Post*, Health (March 28, 2000), p. 8.
22. N. Katherine Hayles, *How We Became Posthuman*, p. 7.

Augmented Reality technology to create "virtual persons" with new interaction techniques:

> The second phase of my thesis will be to develop a software controlling module for **autonomous virtual humans.** *(author's b.f.)* At LIG several researchers are developing virtual humans with synthetic perception modules. I will develop an interaction driven control module to develop applications like Interactive Drama. This control module will let the participants to change [sic] the storyline of a drama.

Conclusions

> In my thesis the main objective is to let human [sic] to interact with autonomous virtual objects in a natural way. This will lead development [sic] of new human machines interfaces for several purposes like, education, entertainment and telepresence.[23]

Already in the 1960's Marshall McLuhan saw that the electronic media had the capacity to reconfigure so extensively "as to change the nature of 'man'."[24] I recall having a brief conversation with Marshall McLuhan at St. Michael's College, Toronto, in the early 1970's when he was nearing the end of his penetrating work on the media. As noted in my earlier book *Toward a Theology of the Body,* there was a serious sadness in his saying that telecommunications separated the human body from the message, sender from receiver, and scenario from reality. When messages are sent into space they are disembodied, said McLuhan. That allows

---

23.   Accessed from the Internet: shttp://ligww.epfl.ch-ssbalcis/Public/proposal.html.
24.   N. Katherine Hayles, *How We Became Posthuman,* p. 34.

the sender to remain aloof and to lose a sense of responsibility for what has been communicated to those receiving and interpreting the message at a distance.[25] He could foresee that electronic media would develop the capacity to "change the nature of man."

This is the heart of the matter, touching the *mystery* that is the human person, with all that this implies concerning creation, relationships, and the completion of human person's fullest realization in the Incarnation of Jesus Christ, the Second Person of the Blessed Trinity. Jesus Christ, the Divine Word, did not come as a "packet of information" sent by wireless transmission. He came in the flesh, in his lived body, revealing the fullness of human potential as total Self-Gift, one who was implicated in bodily realities such as hunger and thirst, suffering and death. All was a loving response to the Will of the Father within the intimacy of Trinitarian relations shared with the Holy Spirit. One of the most frequently cited portions of *Gaudium et spes*, the Dogmatic Constitution on the Church in the Modern World, emphasizes the significance of Jesus Christ's bodily reality in relation to every human person. "In reality it is only in the mystery of the Word made flesh that the mystery of man truly becomes clear."[26] Why is this so? The document states:

> He who is the "image of the invisible God" (Col. 1:15), is himself the perfect man who has restored in the children of Adam that likeness to God which had been disfigured ever since the first sin.... For, by his incarnation, he, the son of God, has in a certain way united himself with each man. He worked with human hands, he

---

25.   See Mary Timothy Prokes, *Toward a Theology of the Body* (Grand Rapids, 1996), pp. 122-123.

26.   *Gaudium et spes*, # 22, in Flannery ed., *The Conciliar and Post Conciliar Documents*.

thought with a human mind. He acted with a human will, and with a human heart he loved. Born of the Virgin Mary, he has truly been made one of us, like to us in all things except sin.[27]

THE FUNDAMENTAL QUESTIONS CONCERNING REAL HUMAN EMBODIMENT

In the introduction to this book I quoted from Michael Heim's book *The Metaphysics of Virtual Reality*, in which he questions whether human nature itself will change. He poses a fundamental question concerning virtual reality: "Will we soon pass some point where we are so altered by our imaginations and inventions as to be unrecognizable to Shakespeare or the writers of the Greek plays?" What theologians must ask, and what the Magisterium must discern is not what a Shakespeare or a Homer might recognize. It is this: *When will there be an alteration of the human body-person so drastic that it will not be recognizable as being made in divine image and likeness?* The second question that follows upon this: *When will there be an alteration of body-person that crosses the boundary of the human in such a way that it no longer can be recognized as being incorporated in the Body of Christ?* From this flows a third question: *When will the fabricated body-individual be so altered that it longer refers to redeemed humanity with a destiny for eternal life?* These are the questions that must be seen as crucial for the Church and for theology in the opening years of the Third Millennium. They refer to signs of the times that are as evident as the drying wind from the south that Jesus cited in his teaching. They are "signs" that must be read within contem-

---

27.   *Gaudium et spes*, #22.

porary theology One can rearrange the theological chairs of Augustine, Thomas, and Duns Scotus, but the slippery deck of faith understanding is already tilting.

The Scriptures, whatever genres are employed in the writings of the various books, deal with the significance of human meaning within the plan of God. To construct an idol is to fashion something that may have eyes but cannot see, ears that cannot hear, a nose that cannot smell. There is a caution in the Scripture also that the human can become like these humanly contrived objects. Psalm 115 has it:

> Ours is the God whose will is sovereign
> in the heavens and on earth,
> whereas their idols, in silver and gold,
> products of human skill,
>
> have mouths, but never speak,
> eyes, but never see,
> ears, but never hear,
> noses, but never smell,
>
> hands, but never touch,
> feet, but never walk,
> and not a sound from their throats.
> Their makers will end up like them,
> and so will anyone who relies on them. (vv. 3-8)

It is not simply a matter of human decisions (whether made by a given individual or group of persons within a society) to determine by preference who is considered human, or who is truly part of the human race. It is a profound issue for faith and theological reflection on faith to ask: *What does it mean to cross the boundary between the human and the non-human, although the basic configuration may look the same, or closely resemble human appearance?*

Redemption is inseparably connected with Jesus Christ, true God and true man. For many centuries, a central issue for theological study and reflection dealt with the meaning of the inseparable union of Jesus Christ's divinity and humanity. Theological debate and magisterial discernment focused on the mysteries of the Incarnation, on Jesus Christ's enduring self-gift in the Paschal Mystery, and the manner in which the liturgical/sacramental life of the Church celebrates these sacred mysteries. How intense were their deliberations and discernment about the *reality* of Jesus Christ's true embodiment as divine person, in union with the Father and the Holy Spirit.

In the beginning years of the Third Millennium of Christianity, the focus has shifted. Standing within the firm foundation of faith and the gifts of theological reflection from the past two millennia, theologians must realize that the paradigm shift that has occurred in the complex of cybernetic/scientific/technological/political practices requires attention precisely as a theological locus. In his Last Discourse, Jesus Christ assured that there was much to be shared, but his core Apostolic leadership was not yet prepared to hear it. If he were to go, however, "Another Advocate," the "Spirit of truth" would be sent. "But when the Spirit of truth comes he will lead you to the complete truth, since he will not be speaking as from himself but will say only what he has learnt; and he will tell you of the things to come.... Everything the Father has is mine; that is why I said: All he tells you will be taken from what is mine." (Jn. 16:13, 15) Repeatedly Jesus urged those close to him not to be afraid, but to trust in the midst of forces that threatened to destroy. He spoke of enduring truth and placed everything into the context of personal relationships, divine and human. He insisted on truthfulness, on what was real.

In his brief public life, Jesus showed through his teaching, but especially through his actions, that the *realities* of creation far exceed what seems possible. His miracles amazed those who witnessed them (often confounding some who thought they knew how a carpenter from Nazareth should conduct himself). As brief as the canonical Gospels are, they show that Jesus also placed his miracles within a larger context: as the divine Person through whom all things were made, he opened to those about him the previously unguessed-at potential of the material creation, both the potential that is within all created beings, but especially the enormous potential within embodied persons.

Long before He promised to give His Body as *real food* and His Blood as *real drink*, Jesus was awakening His disciples to the potency of ordinary bread. His own entry into public mission was marked with an experience concerning bread, and His enduring Paschal Mystery is expressed outwardly through it. In order to receive and understand more deeply the ultimate realization of bread as matter for the Eucharist, it is critical to grow in understanding the potential and meaning of ordinary bread.

Bread and the gift of food and drink taken in communion with those who are beloved is Jesus' particular hallmark. It is not given and received as a "proof" of power, overwhelming those to whom it is given, or requiring payment. The first of Jesus' "signs" according to John was the freely-given miracle of water turned into wine, to save a bridegroom's embarrassment and to provide surpassingly potable wine for a wedding celebration. (See Jn. 2:1-12)

Jesus did not resort to artificiality or flamboyant simulation in his teaching or personal self-gift in the body and the blood. This has proved to be a recurring stumbling block for many who are drawn to him and his message but find the *realities* he promised to be "too much." It can be more comfortable to stop short of those realities and to interpret what Jesus Christ revealed as merely metaphorical, belonging to the realm of the imaginative rather than the actual. It will be necessary to say much more of this in an ensuing chapter dealing with the impact of the virtual on contemporary understandings of food and drink.

The truths of the incarnation, the redemption, and the sacraments are at stake here. A theological debate of the 1960's is informative in this regard. In *The Myth of God Incarnate*, seven theologians and Scripture scholars discussed whether or not the incarnation is essential to Christianity. Frances Young, for example, wrote:

> ...an exclusive claim that the only way of understanding the nature of Jesus is in terms of a unique divine incarnation has been enshrined in authoritative statements traditionally used as tests of orthodoxy. This has caused living witness and faith to appear as improbable scientific fact, and has encouraged arrogant and intolerant attitudes among the faithful. It has also obscured the potential richness and variety of Christological images and insights by tending to subordinate everything to the confession of Jesus as incarnate Son of God.[28]

Another essayist in *The Myth of God Incarnate*, Maurice Wiles, suggested that there are two ways in which "incarnational faith" can be understood: a looser and a stricter way. The "looser" understanding of incarnation, he suggested, means that Christianity approaches God *through* the world, not by escaping from it. In the "stricter" understanding of incarnation, Wiles wrote that it is necessary to affirm that there has been the "incarnation of God in the particular individual Jesus of Nazareth," although, he added, this need not be bound by the specific categories of the definition of the Council of Chalcedon.[29] Wiles then asked: could there

---

28.   Frances Young, "A Cloud of Witnesses," in *The Myth of God Incarnate*, John Hick ed. (Philadelphia, 1977), p. 13.

be a Christianity without the *stricter* understanding of incarnation? The terms "Christianity" and "incarnation" have become virtually synonymous, he wrote, but "There is nothing intellectually perverse in drawing a distinction between the two concepts and asking whether it might be possible to have one without the other."[30]

In other words, in the sophisticated contemporary world, is it possible to hold that God has truly become man? Or, can there be a fluidity of interpretations as to what it means that Christians affirm "incarnation"? Michael Goulder, another essayist in the collection entitled *The Myth of God Incarnate*, noted that the Christian faith has become intellectually disreputable in the eyes of philosophers because "it no longer asserts anything." Our forebears believed things accessible to all in the Bible, he said, but now:

> We don't believe in hell (most of us) or the devil or verbal inspiration, and when such ideas are derided we join in the laughter: "did you really think we believed that" we say. Even when the incarnation, or divine providence, or almost any view of the atonement is derided, the Christian is often found to be joining in too, perhaps rather uncomfortably: did you really think we believed that? "Well," says the philosopher, "it sounds as if your faith is pretty elastic: can you get by without the resurrection, or the historicity of Jesus? Aren't you really a humanist, but without the honesty to say so?"[31]

---

29.   Maurice Wiles, "Christianity without Incarnation?" in *The Myth of God Incarnate*, p. 1.
30.   Maurice Wiles, "Christianity without Incarnation?" p. 2.
31.   Michael Goulder, "Jesus, The Man of Universal Destiny," in *The Myth of God Incarnate,* p. 48.

One has to admire the forthrightness of these scholars, already presaging in the 1970's the ways in which freedom to interpret terms and underlying truths of faith intersected with the explosive development of virtual reality and the attendant fluidity of interpretation. If some theologians suppose that bodily realities are open to individual interpretation, some who are involved in the theory and development of virtual realities recognize the significance involved. Michael Heim, for example, acknowledged profound issues concerning the interface between human persons and computers *where spirit seems to migrate from real body to a world of total representation. Information and images float through the mind without grounding in bodily experience.* He has noted:

> Our bodily existence stands at the forefront of our personal identity and individuality. Both law and morality recognize the physical body as something of a fence, an absolute boundary, establishing and protecting our privacy. Now the computer network simply brackets the physical presence of the participants, by either omitting or simulating corporeal immediacy.... Bodily contact becomes optional; you need never stand face-to-face with other members of the virtual community. You can live your own separate existence without ever physically meeting another person.[32]

Heim is very direct. At the computer interface, he writes, "the spirit migrates from the body to a world of total representation." Here, images and information float through "the Platonic mind without a grounding in bodily experience. You can lose your humanity at the throw of the dice."[33] It

---

32.   Michael Heim, *The Metaphysics of Virtual Reality*, p. 100.
33.   Michael Heim, *The Metaphysics of Virtual Reality*, p. 101.

will be essential to return to the theological meaning of *interface* in the following chapter.

Recall how N. Katherine Hayles states that there is a point of view in the posthuman world that has definite assumptions. First, **information pattern has privilege over material instantiation.** This means that the body is considered merely a biological substrate, an accident of history rather than the inevitable expression of human life. Second, in the posthuman view, **consciousness** is the basis of human identity. Third, this view considers the body as "the original **prosthesis** that we all learn to manipulate." In a process that begins before birth, other prostheses continue to replace the "real body." Fourth, the posthuman view "configures human being so that it can be seamlessly articulated with intelligent machines."[34]

Literature dealing with research on virtual reality sometimes speaks of perfecting the interface between human and machine, of attempting to facilitate the interflow there, and overcoming the boundaries between them. If the human person is considered to be essentially "**information**," the lived body becomes superfluous, an obstacle to be overcome. According to Hayles, Marvin Minsky has suggested in a public lecture that it will soon be possible "to extract human memories from the brain and import them, intact and unchanged, to computer disks. The clear implication is that if we can become the information we have constructed, we can achieve effective immortality."[35] An important fact emerges from this thinking: It is not *all* materiality that is dismissed as irrelevant. It is, rather, an ever-smaller quantity of matter that transmits and holds packets of information. The electronically configured containers are in flux, and are

---

34.   See N. Katherine Hayles, *How We Became Posthuman*, pp. 2-3.
35.   N. Katherine Hayles, *How We Became Posthuman*, p. 13.

prepared ever more swiftly in compact forms. They are disposable, impersonal, already *passé* by the time of installation in receptors. They are simply placeholders for a process.

In such a view, since the process is dealing only with "packets of information," there is no need for a soul. Ray S. Anderson questions whether or not the concept of a human soul has disappeared in molecular biology, clinical psychology, and brain scans that are computer-driven. He ponders whether the disappearance of "soul" indicates that the world has "come of age," or if we are lost and our souls are doing the searching. "What gives rise to our deepest religious insights but can also plunge us into the depths of guilt and despair?" he asks.[36] Since many contemporary theologians are uncomfortable with the dualistic, abstract notion of body/soul deriving from Descartes, Anderson says, many of them reject the concept *soul* as a distinct entity and will often use "the word 'spirit' as a virtual synonym for the 'soul' but without the implication, or embarrassment, of having to define or locate the 'soul' as a component of human nature."[37] In his own work, Ray S. Anderson explains that

---

36.   Ray S. Anderson, "On Being Human: The Spiritual Saga of a Creaturely Soul," in *Whatever Happened to the Soul? Scientific and Theological Portraits of Human Nature*, Warren S. Brown, Nancey Murphy and H. Newton Malony, eds. (Minneapolis, 1998), p. 175. Anderson quotes Thomas Moore, *Care of the Soul: A Guide for Cultivating Depth and Sacredness in Everyday Life* (New York, 1992), xi: "The great malady of the twentieth century, implicated in all of our troubles and affecting us individually and socially, is 'loss of soul.' When soul is neglected, it doesn't just go away; it appears symptomatically in obsessions, addictions, violence, and loss of meaning. Our temptation is to isolate these symptoms or to try to eradicate them one by one; but the root problem is that we have lost our wisdom about the soul, even our interest in it."

37.   Ray S. Anderson, "On Being Human: The Spiritual Saga of a Creaturely Soul," pp. 176-177.

he considers the terms *body, soul* and *spirit* as describing the phenomena of human existence, "not susceptible to an analytical depiction of human nature."[38] He sees concern for the human soul as a concern for the quality of life "at its deepest core of our existential life," including the ecology of physical life in the cosmos, the manifesting of the divine image, and humans being what they are "by the breath of God's Spirit."[39] As Nancey Murphy points out in the opening chapter of *Whatever Happened to the Human Soul,* the authors, including Anderson, wanted to grapple with the view of many contemporary philosophers and scientists who suppose that "the person is but one substance—a physical body," and who see that human faculties once attributed to the soul are now perceived as simply functions of the brain. Murphy writes that each chapter of their book develops a view of person termed "non-reductive physicalism":

> "Physicalism" signals our agreement with the scientists and philosophers who hold that it is not necessary to postulate a second metaphysical entity, the soul or mind, to account for human capacities and distinctiveness. "Non-reductive" indicates our rejection of contemporary philosophical views that say that the person is "nothing but" a body. That is, many physicalist accounts of the person are also reductive; they aim to show that human behavior can be *exhaustively* explained by means of genetics or neurobiology. So the difficult issue is to explain how we can claim that we *are* our bodies, yet without denying the "higher" capacities that we think of as being essential for our humanness: rationality, emotion, morality, free

---

38.   Ray S. Anderson, "On Being Human: The Spiritual Saga of a Creaturely Soul," p. 182.

39.   See Ray S. Anderson, "On Being Human: The Spiritual Sage of a Creaturely Soul," p. 194.

will, and, most important, the capacity to be in relationship with God.[40]

The attempt to bring about such a "non-reductive" synthesis shows the struggle to assimilate contemporary scientific and philosophical perspectives with faith in God. It is
the seriousness of effort in works such as *Whatever Happened
to the Human Soul?* (not their conclusions) that points to the
significance of theological issues that directly touch upon the
integrity of the living body-person.

STAMPED MATRIX OR DIVINE IMAGE AND LIKENESS?

Entertainment films, a prime example of virtual reality
in themselves, also currently deal with exotic developments
of "the virtual." A film that has become a kind of classic in
this regard is *The Matrix*, in which the character "Morpheus"
immerses a computer hacker, "Neo," into a computer-generated world. Early in the film narrative, Neo hesitatingly asks,
"Right now we are inside a computer program?" The reply:
"Is that so hard to believe? Your appearance now is what we
call residual self-image, a mental projection of your digital
self." Neo then stammers, "This, this isn't REAL." Morpheus
replies:

> What is real? How do you define real? If you are talk-
> ing about what you feel, what you smell, what you taste
> and see, then "real" is simply electrical signals interpreted
> by your brain. This is the world that you knew as it was at
> the end of the twentieth century. It exists now only as part

---

40.   Nancey Murphy, "Human Nature: Historical, Scientific, and
       Religious Issues," in *Whatever Happened to the Human Soul*, p. 2.

of a neural interactive simulator, what we call "the Matrix."

In one sequence of *The Matrix*, Neo is shown what resemble embryos connected to a swirl of cables. He is told that these are "endless fields where human beings are no longer born but grow." He is assured also that, "As long as the Matrix exists, the human will never be free." Less than a decade after *The Matrix* presented images of virtual embryos being raised in rows like laboratory crops, the United States Congress was debating the issue of mass-producing embryos that would serve as donors of stem cells and subsequently be destroyed in the early weeks of their existence. *The Matrix* ends with a message. An ominous voice is heard:

> I know you're out there. I can feel you now. I know you're afraid. You're afraid of "us." You're afraid of change. I don't know the future. I didn't come to tell you how this is going to end. I came here to tell you how it's going to *begin*. I'm going to hang up now and then I'm going to tell these people what you don't want...a world without *you*. A world without rules and controls, without borders. A world where *anything* is possible. Where we go from there is the choice I leave to you.

Choices *are* being made that presume a world "where anything is possible." *The Matrix* concludes with a challenge analogous to the one given to Eve by the serpent in the Garden of Genesis, Chapter Two. Both concern the lived body and future possibilities. It has been easy, until quite recently, to dismiss "anything is possible technologically" as imaginative science fiction. No more. Several years ago, in a World Economic Forum in Davos, Switzerland, a scientist confidently stated that robots which will be smarter and more durable than humans will eventually take over the world. If they choose, they will make humans their pets. He also commented that it will be possible to download the "essence" of persons, either onto disks or into robots, making "life eternal" possible on earth.

Observations such as these, which emerge from scientific gatherings, are no longer the dream projections of novelists and film producers. They are seriously intended and thoughtfully heard. They are theologically significant because they touch upon the central affirmations of the *Fides quae*, the deposit of faith, and upon what it means to be a body-person in a divinely created universe, called to live eternally in intimate union with Persons of the Trinity. There is no "virtual redemption." St. Paul reminded the Corinthians: "Your body, you know, is the temple of the Holy Spirit, who is in you since you received him from God. You are not your own property; you have been bought and paid for. That is why you should use your body for the glory of God." (I Cor. 6: 19-20)

It is of great significance that scientists and technicians who work toward made-to-order posthumans raise the deepest issues concerning faith. What does it mean to be a human person? Why does Genesis affirm that male and female together are image and likeness of God? If Divine Persons are perichoretic *relationships* as their very being, what does the *analogy of being* mean in regard to human fabrications that would meld human and animal, human and computer ware? What is the enduring significance of matter in eternal life, transformed forever after the resurrection of the incarnate Christ? How is the Last Discourse of John's Gospel to be read in light of the call to be indwelt by the Holy Spirit?

As Christians live into the Third Millennium, current research and the vigorous affirmations about the reformulating of human life must be taken seriously. It is not a matter of dismissing them; rather, they evoke the questions that must be pursued at this moment of history. It is theologically important to ask: *What is emerging in humanity in new dimensions that reveals a hunger for the realities that find their full realization in Christ?* How will the Holy Spirit overshadow the theological task at hand so that there can be an advance in reflection that is consonant to meet the issues currently proposed by scientists and technicians? Some assessors of future planning assume that the possibilities envisioned for a "posthuman world" and the technological expertise expended to achieve them are inevitable and can no longer be contained. Since the splitting of the atom, there is no longer the human possibility of containing forces of energy that exceed in magnitude, temperature and intensity what preceded them. The breaking of containment boundaries is now assumed to apply to *every* human capacity. Joel Garreau writes that the superheroes of past decades, from Superman and Wonder Woman to Spiderman reveal foreshadowings of technologies that either already exist or are in the process of being engineered. He asserts that no one even "blinks" when the Olympic Committees planning for the 2008 games in China are concerned about "gene doping." Through experiments with mice, it has already been shown how genetically engineered mice have shown a muscle mass increase as high as three hundred percent. Garreau cites the opinion of Max More, president of the Extropy Institute (which pioneers the acceleration of technology and "transhumanism") that "The remaining human future is 25 years or 50 years."[41] Citing authors such as Ray Kurzweil, Christine Peterson and Gregory Stock, who address the future of humanity, Joel Garreau writes:

---

41.   Joel Garreau, "The Next Generation: Biotechnology May Make Superhero Fantasy a Reality," in *The Washington Post*, April 26, 2002, p. C4.

What none of these authors is disputing is the notion that "as exponential growth continues to accelerate into the first half of the twenty-first century," as Kurweil puts it, "it will appear to explode into infinity, at least from the limited and linear perspective of contemporary humans," resulting in "technological change so rapid and so profound that it represents a rupture in the fabric of human history.... What human beings are is a species that has undergone a cultural and technological evolution, and it's the nature of evolution that it accelerates, and that its powers grow exponentially, and that's what we're talking about.... What is unique about human beings is our ability to create abstract models and to use these mental models to understand the world and do something about it.... This ability to scale up the power of our own civilization is what's unique about human beings."[42]

Note carefully Kurweil's assumption that the uniqueness of human beings is the ability to create abstract models. This, however, is a function that is also characteristic of computer-generated programs. Gregory Stock, author of *Redesigning Humans: Our Inevitable Genetic Future*, holds that the utilization of genetic engineering in the reworking of human biology is something that religious groups and governments will not be able to stop.[43]

REAL BODY AS LOCUS FOR THE SACRAMENTAL

Paradoxically, the commercial and entertainment industries, immersed in so much that is virtual, appeal to images

---

42. Joel Garreau, "The Next Generation: Biotechnology May Make Superhero Fantasy a Reality," p. C4.
43. Joel Garreau, "The Next Generation," p. C4.

of the real, the personal, the sacramental and sacred to sell their products. Several decades ago, Coca-Cola marketed its thirst-quencher as "The Real Thing." The sobriquet "The Real Thing" (whether consciously or unconsciously recognized by developers of the slogan) has roots that tap into the depths of sacramental life, but especially the Eucharist.

There is a basic sacramental principle termed *"res et sacramentum."* It refers to both the seen and the unseen aspects of the sacraments. *Sacramentum* designates the "outward sign" of a sacrament, the material elements such as water, oil, bread and wine, and the form of words that formally impart sacraments. The *res*, however, means the "real thing" or personal grace of the sacrament, its deepest efficaciousness. They are "at one." They involve what is termed "Real Symbol." The outward signs (such as pouring of water in Baptism, in the name of the Father, the Son and the Holy Spirit) indeed effect what is signified because, as the Fathers of the Church affirmed, *it is the living Christ who is present and is baptizing efficaciously.* Likewise, in the Eucharist, the summit of every possibility in the liturgy and the life of the universe, it is the **real living self-gift of Jesus in His Body and Blood** that is present through the outward signs.

How often through the history of Christian faith there has been misunderstanding of the sacramental truth of *res et sacramentum.* The term has often been confused with magic, with mere outward ritual, or with gross misunderstanding of the body. Different ages have grappled with a variety of denials and aberrations concerning sacramental mysteries, but our own moment of time brings new challenges. Just as many in earlier centuries thought that the truths of faith were in danger of being destroyed by persons and events of their time, so it may seem now. Wherever there is confusion about the *realities* of sacramental life, or outright denial of their enduring meaning, the immediate concern of both the Magisterium and theologians is essential. Along with this concern echoes the quiet insistence of Jesus that also must be heard afresh: "Do not be afraid.... Can you not read the signs of the times?" Theologically, to miss the most significant signs of the times is to dawdle in superficial responses to those times.

As assertions are made that human beings owe their uniqueness to the ability to create abstract models and employ them, and that the forging of posthuman models is "unstoppable" by a church or government, theological responsibility increases for discerning "what the Spirit is saying to the Churches." A term frequently used by those who develop applications of virtual reality is *interface*. It is important to consider it briefly within this introductory work on virtual reality, since it provides an entry into issues that concern the basic faith reality of *presence*.

3

VIRTUAL REALITY AND REAL PRESENCE

*T*he terms *presence* and *interface* are crucial in the exploration of theological issues associated with virtual reality. Since neither term is univocal in meaning, it is important to ask initially: from the stance of Catholic theology, what does it mean to be "personally present"? How is presence manifest? How is *interface* related to presence? Since the purpose here is to probe major ways in which virtual reality and its applications touch upon "faith seeking understanding," the basic concern is this: how does "the virtual" impinge upon *personal* presence and *personal* interface?

Some initial distinctions need to be made between "being present" and "presence." To be present in space and time involves some influence, some effect, whether there is immediate personal awareness of it or not. In that broad sense, even inanimate beings or minute organisms are "present" and have effects in daily life. *The size of a being and its perception by the senses are not the determining factors of presence.* Often, it is a harmful agent of some kind that raises awareness of what is present but has not yet been perceived. Recall the anthrax spores sent through the United States mail in 2001: these minuscule lethal agents were present, but one would not describe them as a "presence." Human interactions also require distinctions in regard to presence. Large numbers of people gather in ballparks and concert halls and airports. There is a necessary crowding together that, for the most part, excludes a sense of personal presence. *Presence* cannot simply be equated with immediate location or physical proximity. Only in a radically diminished sense could one say that hundreds of people waiting at a subway stop are "present" to one another. While these are necessary aspects of human life, such gatherings are not of prime concern here. In the context of this theological exploration, *presence* refers to that range of meaning that involves an actual, *personal, relational* being-there that has a positive or negative effect.

In the contemporary, so-called "Posthuman" period, there is a fundamental questioning of a need for actual personal presence. N. Katherine Hayles, for example, reflecting on her experience of *VR* simulations at the Human Interface Technology Laboratory and elsewhere, says that she can attest to a "disorienting, exhilarating effect" in feeling that one's "subjectivity is dispersed throughout the cybernetic circuit.... Questions about presence and absence do not yield much leverage in this situation, for the avatar both is and is not present, just as the user both is and is not inside the screen."[1] Hayles notes the difference between producing a script on a typewriter and working with a "text-as-flickering image" on a computer. In the latter, pattern and randomness are "more real, more relevant, and more powerful than presence and absence."[2]

If presence has diminished in significance in the realm of virtual reality, the term *interface*, which is commonly

---

1.   N. Katherine Hayles, *How We Became Posthuman*, p. 27.

2.   N. Katherine Hayles, *How We Became Posthuman*, p. 26.

employed in the literature of this expanding field of research and experimentation, may prove to be a helpful bridge when probing theological issues arising from *VR*. In fact, as will be suggested later, *interface* may constitute a positive encounter point between theology and virtual reality. While the term interface designates a fluid boundary point for *VR*, it also indicates a growing human hunger to exceed ordinary experience of limited presence.

Like *presence*, the word *interface* has complex meanings. According to *Webster's*, "interface" can denote a *surface* that forms a common boundary of two bodies or two spaces; it can also designate a *place* where independent systems can meet, act upon, or influence each other. Or, an interface can denote a *means of communication or interaction* at a mutual boundary. Finally, the term interface can refer to a *connection point*, such as that which joins a computer with a machine. These are basic, general meanings of the word.

In the current literature concerning virtual reality, the term *interface* covers a wide range of meanings. It can simply designate the surface of a computer monitor, or it can describe the fluid boundary between reality and virtuality. In *Narrative as Virtual Reality*, Marie-Laure Ryan cites a number of authors who anticipate the overcoming of boundaries to the extent that there will no longer be a need for mediation between reality and virtual reality. She writes:

> "Virtual reality" is not just the ultimate medium, it is the ultimate interface metaphor.... The dream of an optimal interface is the dream of a command language naturally fitted to the task at hand. This means that in VR symbolic code must disappear, at least in those areas in which it can be more efficiently replaced by physical actions.[3]

There is a search for what is termed "postsymbolic communication" in a "postliterate era," a language without symbols in which "people will build a shared reality and minds will become transparent to each other."[4] The desire to overcome boundaries in communication extends much farther still for some in the field of *VR*. Virtual environments can be considered workshops for "do-it-yourself bodies serving as manifestations of do-it-yourself identities."[5] Ryan writes:

> The possibility of redesigning our bodies and becoming something or somebody else is indeed a central theme in Jaron Lanier's 1988 description of the Home Reality Engine: "The computer that's running the Virtual Reality will use your body's movements to control whatever body you choose to have in Virtual Reality, which might be human or might be something quite different. You might very well be a mountain range or a galaxy or a pebble on the floor. A piano..." (Zhai, *Get Real*, 177).[6]

Ryan points out that some media theorists praise the technology employed in *VR* for teaching relativity of point of view since it allows a user to have an experience of what it is like to be someone or something else, and serves as a means of self-discovery. Appealing to several appraisers of *VR*, Ryan notes that for complete immersion, the user needs to go beyond the framed screen of a monitor. In real *VR*, it is not a matter of a framed "world-within-a-world." She quotes Gabriel D. Ofeisch who observed, "As long as you can see the screen, you're not in VR. When the screen disappears, and you can see an imaginary screen...then you are in VR."[7]

---

3. Marie-Laure Ryan, *Narrative as Virtual Reality*, p. 58.
4. Marie-Laure Ryan, *Narrative as Virtual Reality*, p. 59.
5. Marie-Laure Ryan, *Narrative as Virtual Reality*, p. 61.
6. Marie-Laure Ryan, *Narrative as Virtual Reality*, p. 61.
7. See Ryan, *Narrative as Virtual Reality*, p. 58, for further references.

Here a boundary is crossed. The user experiences a passing over and then a return to "reality." Some may argue that this also occurs in dreams. During sleep, however, dreams arise from the depths of the unconscious. Dreams are an integrating factor within the person and are not artificially induced and/or fashioned technologically from without. In advanced forms of virtual reality, on the other hand, the user can cross an interface in various ways. For some, it involves the devising of a virtual environment in which there is the "crossing over" into an avatar (a kind of alternate body in a virtual world) where it is possible to interact with others who also have crossed over that boundary into avatars.

Benjamin Woolley, in the introductory chapter of *Virtual Worlds,* asks how one can keep a clear distinction between reality and fantasy "when the unreal is continually being realized." He points out that for many centuries, *reality* was the subject of philosophers. Now, "reality is no longer secure, no longer something we can simply assume to be there."[8] Humanity has come to a way of "creating" what in past times seemed impossibilities, from fat-free-fat to "the actual creation of any world you could ever want or imagine—fantastical, fabulous, terrifying, infinite, enclosed, utopian, Stygian."[9] This is typified to some extent already in the Disney "Lands" that feature not only simulated versions of foreign cultures, but also imaginary beings that have no counterparts in reality. Daily life in so-called developed nations of the West is already immersed in "artificial reality."

Woolley exemplifies this by citing the reflections of Jean Baudrillard concerning elements of the Gulf War. Baudrillard reflected on the way some pilots described their experi-

---

8.   Benjamin Woolley, *Virtual Worlds: A Journey in Hype and Hyper-reality* (Oxford, UK, 1992), p. 5.
9.   Benjamin Woolley, *Virtual Worlds*, p. 7.

ences in the war.[10] One fighter pilot said that he felt like a young athlete who just completed a football match. Another exclaimed how Baghdad under fire looked like a Christmas tree or a Fourth of July party. Tellingly, one pilot said, "It was exactly like the movies."[11] The last of these comments exemplifies how easy it has become to cross the interface between the reality of war and artificially contrived images of war projected on a screen.

On the other hand, who has not been moved by great theater, photography, or films that express truth artistically? It is the indiscriminate merging of life and the art that imitates life (the loss of the actual in the contrived—or even the *preference* for the contrived) that is concerned here. It is relatively common to hear someone describe actual roses as "so beautiful, you'd think they were artificial!" implying that artificial blossoms have greater perfection than living roses. Even in such cases, however, the comparison itself is still based in a reality: the organic, living flower.

There is a new and pervasive kind of virtuality, however, that already exceeds the imitation of an original reality. Woolley compares the great migration that took place from farm to factory in the industrial revolution to the migration that has taken place in the post industrial world: "from factory to fantasy." In some cases, he points out, copies, or altered "copies" become more desirable, and are judged "more perfect" than the originals they supposedly represent. For example, Leonardo da Vinci painted his "Last Supper"on the refectory wall of a monastery in Milan. The technique he employed was experimental and did not survive well with time. So, more recent artists have "reproduced" it in wax and other media, attempting to make it more pleas-

---

10.   See Benjamin Woolley, *Virtual Worlds*, pp. 190ff.

11.   Benjamin Woolley, *Virtual Worlds*, p. 191.

ing to the eye. The original is now considered by some to be inadequate when compared with the vibrant copies.[12]

> For postmodernist critics, the *Last Supper* reproductions and Polaroid replicas are symptomatic of mounting fear of losing the reality that sustained the modern world in the absence of religious authority. Auction house prices, tourism, theme parks and even wars are ways we have developed for fooling ourselves that such a reality still exists. *We are like cartoon characters who have walked off a cliff edge and, still suspended in the air, have suddenly realized that there is nothing beneath us.* This is the 'crisis' of postmodernity, and it is technology that has produced it.[13] *(italics mine)*

It is evident that an indiscriminate crossing of the interface between the real and the artificial profoundly affects matters of faith and the theological understanding of faith. If sign and symbol, and the realities they signify, come to be considered irrelevant in a "posthuman world," the basic truths of faith are at stake. Sacred Scripture conveys divinely revealed truths through writings that are laced with signs and symbols having a direct relation to enduring truths. Concrete signs and symbols are an enduring form of humanity's interface with divine revelation. Sacramental signs express the efficaciousness of divine action and grace. The *Catechism of the Catholic Church* states that "A sacramental celebration is woven from signs and symbols...their meaning is rooted in the work of creation and in human culture, specified by the events of the Old Covenant and fully revealed in the person and work of Christ."[14] Ensuing paragraphs of the *Catechism* describe the manner in which the Liturgy is celebrated,

---

12.   See Benjamin Wooley, *Virtual Worlds*, p. 203.
13.   Benjamin Woolley, *Virtual Worlds*, p. 204.

emphasizing that signs and symbols are integral to it: signs of human interaction in the world, signs of visible creation, ritual signs which endure through the ages, signs of the Covenant which are taken up by Christ.

Since human persons are at once body and spirit, spiritual realities are perceived through physical signs and symbols. A human person needs "signs and symbols to communicate with others, through language, gestures, and actions. The same holds true for his relationship with God."[15] The efficacious reception of grace comes through signs and symbols.

A sacramental celebration is indeed a sacred interface: a *place* of meeting between divine and human persons. It is a *means* and a *connection point*, enabling members of the Church to know that the Risen Jesus Christ is efficaciously present, acting on their behalf. The *Catechism* expresses this clearly. It recalls how the Lord Jesus used physical signs and symbolic gestures, giving new meaning to the deeds and signs of the Old Covenant, "above all to the Exodus and the Passover, for he himself is the meaning of all these signs." (#1151)

> Since Pentecost, it is through the sacramental signs of his Church that the Holy Spirit carries on the work of sanctification. The sacraments of the Church do not abolish but purify and integrate all the richness of the signs and symbols of the cosmos and of social life. (#1152)

> The liturgical celebration involves signs and symbols relating to creation (candles, water, fire), human life (washing, anointing, breaking bread) and the history of

---

14.   *Catechism of the Catholic Church*, Second Edition (Libreria Editrice Vaticana, 1997), #1145, p. 296.

15.   *Catechism of the Catholic Church*, #1146.

salvation (the rites of the Passover). Integrated into the world of faith and taken up by the power of the Holy Spirit, these cosmic elements, human rituals, and gestures of remembrance of God become bearers of the saving and sanctifying action of Christ. (#1189)

In what can be termed a sacramental interface, there is a crossing over that is not artificially devised nor changeable in meaning according to momentary creativity. The core signs and symbols of faith endure. They are not arbitrarily chosen. Thus, in the Dogmatic Constitution on the Liturgy, *Sacrosanctum Concilium*, the Council Fathers clarified the care that must be taken in renewing the sacramental life of the Church, stating clearly that liturgical services are not private functions. Competent ecclesial authority determines the regulations that safeguard integral celebrations of the sacred liturgy. "Therefore, no other person, not even a priest, may add, remove, or change anything in the liturgy on his own authority."[16]

These magisterial clarifications may sound unfamiliar to many in contemporary Western cultures who are already immersed in the fluid patterns of virtual reality. If the enduring meaning of signs and symbols is considered irrelevant, and concomitantly, if real presence and real absence are considered irrelevant, the core truths of faith and divine-human relationship can also come to be considered irrelevant.

REAL SYMBOL

A cornerstone of sacramental theology is enunciated in the term "Real Symbol." It expresses succinctly the meaning

---

16.   *The Constitution on the Sacred Liturgy*, in *Vatican Council II: The Conciliar and Post Conciliar Documents*, Austin Flannery, ed., #22, pp. 9-10.

of sacramental symbolism. As noted above, sacraments are "woven" of signs and symbols. Sacramental theology closely relates three terms: *sacramentum tantum* (sacramental signs only); *res et sacramentum* (the reality and the sacramental signs); and *res tantum* (the reality only). This threefold designation carefully shows a progression of entry into the depths of sacramental reality. The term *sacramentum tantum*, or the sacramental signs only, refers to palpable material: things such as fragrant oil, water, bread and wine and the words which relate how Christ is present and acting efficaciously in each sacrament. The *res et sacramentum*, or symbolic reality (efficacious presence *with* the sacramental signs) refers to the unity of the outward signs and the inner reality, which disclose how the living, present Christ is acting on behalf of the recipient. Finally, the *res tantum*, or reality only, designates the specific efficacious results given to the recipients of each of the sacraments.

The *res* or reality is crucial. Sacraments not only sign a gracious action of God: they really bear the efficacious presence and action of Christ. The ultimate Real Symbol is that of the Eucharist, in which Jesus Christ, through the imminent effective presence of the Holy Spirit, continues to give himself actually as saving self-gift in his real body, blood, soul and divinity. Bernard Leeming writes:

> By the end of the twelfth century a triple distinction was universally recognized and accepted:
>
> The outward rite, by which bread and wine are consecrated, or the appearances of bread and wine after consecration: this is the *sacramentum tantum*, merely a sacrament.
>
> The body and blood present under the appearances of bread and wine: this is called the Blessed Sacrament, and is a reality which is also a sacrament, a *res et sacramentum*.

The body and blood of Christ are truly present, but they point to something further, to spiritual nourishment and union with Christ in his Mystical Body.

The ultimate thing pointed to, signified, the *res tantum*, which is the unity of the members of the Church with Christ, the growth in grace and charity.[17]

The Dogmatic Constitution on the Liturgy, *Sacrosanctum Concilium*, speaks of Christ's enduring presence in the Church, particularly in liturgical celebrations. Those who wrote this document of the Second Vatican Council took care to emphasize the *reality* of Christ's presence in the sacrifice of the Mass. They cited the twenty-second session of the Council of Trent which concerns the Church's doctrine on the Mass, in which the earlier Council had stated: "the same now offering, through the ministry of priests, who formerly offered himself on the cross."[18] In Article #7 of *Sacrosanctum Concilium*, the Fathers of the Second Vatican Council also distinguished the various ways in which Christ is present in the Eucharist and all of the sacraments. Christ is present not only in the sacred species but also in the person of the celebrant and the Word. He is present when the church prays and sings, as He promised, saying that where two or three gather, He is there. (Cf. Matt. 18:20)

The words *Real Presence* succinctly express Catholic belief in the true, living presence of Jesus Christ in the Eucharist. Everything hinges on the enduring genuineness of both the reality of the Risen Lord and His presence. Moreover, the very possibility of Real Presence in the Eucharist

---

17. Bernard Leeming, *Principles of Sacramental Theology*, sixth impression (Westminster, Maryland, 1963), p. 255.

18. See *Sacrosanctum Concilium*, #7.

depends upon the *Real Incarnation* of the Second Person of the Trinity. Were Jesus Christ not truly the Second Person of the Trinity, there would be no Real Incarnation, and hence no redemption. If Jesus Christ is not risen from the dead, the sacramental life of the Church would not only be futile—it would be untruthful. St. Paul addressed this in his First Letter to the Corinthians:

> Now if Christ raised from the dead is what has been preached, how can some of you be saying that there is no resurrection of the dead? If there is no resurrection of the dead, Christ himself cannot have been raised, and if Christ has not been raised then our preaching is useless and your believing it is useless; indeed, we are shown up as witnesses who have committed perjury before God, because we swore in evidence before God that he had raised Christ to life. For if the dead are not raised, Christ has not been raised, and if Christ has not been raised, you are still in your sins. And what is more serious, all who have died in Christ have perished. If our hope in Christ has been for this life only, we are the most unfortunate of all people. (I Cor. 15:12-19)

The most profound level and meaning of symbol is the total unity between what is outwardly, perceptibly symbolized and the true presence of what is being symbolized. As Karl Rahner wrote, "...the Logos, as Son of the Father, is truly, in his humanity as such, the revelatory symbol in which the Father enunciates himself, in this Son, to the world—revelatory, because the symbol renders present what is revealed."[19] Just as Jesus Christ is really present, Body and Soul in the Eucharistic Presence, recipients of the sacraments

---

19.   Karl Rahner, "The Theology of the Symbol," in *Theological Investigations IV,* trans. Kevin Smyth (Baltimore, 1966), p. 239.

must also be truly present to the sacramental celebration. Sacraments are for the living and may not be administered to the dead.

The understanding of authentic presence is foundational to Catholic faith. That is why N. Katherine Hayles' observations concerning presence and absence pose theological questions associated with advances in the field of virtual reality. She describes the technological shift that occurs in *VR* when the user's sensory system is put into a direct feedback loop with the computer. The illusion is created that "the user is *inside* the computer."[20] She notes that the "relevant boundaries" are defined less by the skin and more by the feedback loops which connect the body and the simulation in what she terms a technobio-integrated circuit. "Questions about presence and absence do not yield much leverage in this situation," she says, "for the avatar both is and is not present, just as the user both is and is not inside the screen."[21]

The day-to-day world that is now awash with flickering images on computer monitors, television sets, and movie theater screens can dull awareness regarding the importance of real presence in real bodies. Hayles relates that Sherry Turkle, through research on persons participating in multi-user computer games, found that virtual technologies have a "riptide of reverse influence" and do affect how *real* life is perceived. One of Turkle's respondents remarked, "Reality is not my best window."[22] Boundaries between the real and the simulated are not simply blurred; rather, there is a kind of crossing-over into the realm of the simulated that can result in its being preferred to that which is real. The artificial and

20.   N. Katherine Hayles, *How We Became Posthuman*, p. 27.
21.   N. Katherine Hayles, *How We Became Posthuman*, p. 27.
22.   See N. Katherine Hayles, *How We Became Posthuman*, p. 27.

the simulated certainly characterize much of the entertainment industry. Increasingly, these characteristics permeate the socio-economic fabric of the "first-world." Money, for example, says Hayles is experienced increasingly as "informational patterns stored in computer banks" rather than actually present cash. Of greater import, as *in vitro* fertilization and maternal surrogacy demonstrate, it is "informational genetic patterns" rather than physical presence/intercourse that determine who the "legitimate" parents are.[23] Presence and absence, on the other hand, are traits associated with bodied reality, with effective signs and symbols, with communication and communion. To touch any one of these traits is to touch human personhood and human relationship to Divine Persons.

TRANSPARENT BOUNDARIES

When human endeavor achieves an innovative breakthrough, it is important to ask: what good may come from it? What gifts and responsibilities may be surging into consciousness, despite distortions in the application of an innovative tool? To read the signs of the times requires such questioning. The twentieth century marked, for example, the initial human capacity 1) to release the immense power in an atom; 2) to identify the DNA spiral and the sequences in the human genome; 3) to leap on the surface of the moon; and 4) to digitalize multiple forms of communication on minuscule bits of matter. These, along with other prodigious breakthroughs of the last century, have simultaneously marked blessing and calamity. Each represents the passing of boundaries formerly thought impregnable. Faith, enduring

---

23.   See N. Katherine Hayles, *How We Became Posthuman*, p. 27.

to the end of the world, must grapple with their meaning, assured that "...Yahweh's plans hold good for ever, the intentions of his heart, from age to age." (Ps. 33:11)

It was suggested earlier in this chapter that the desire to overcome boundaries (although "acted out" perversely at times) reveals a longing that erupts from the depths of the human person. It is a longing that can only be partially fulfilled in present life, but anticipates true realization in risen life. The greater a given potential and gift, the more radical is its misuse or perversion, as the first chapters of Genesis exemplify. If forms of virtual reality seem to supercede the need for presence, for bodily and material reality, they depart from core aspects of Christian faith. The comparison can be drawn between this dismissal of human creatureliness and the response of humanity at its fountainhead, as depicted in Genesis 1-3. What can be garnered positively from the *VR* pursuit of a condition in which communication and union have no boundaries is *the human capacity to transcend*, to pass back and forth freely. As suggested above, Marie-Laure Ryan's commentary on an anticipated "post-literate era" bears particular significance for theology. Through language without symbols, she says, "...people will build a shared reality and minds will become transparent to each other."[24] The desire to attain transparency of mind to others (while presently associated with computerized, simulated scenarios, and contrived mental intimacy) manifests a far deeper surge from the human depths. Thus, Lanier and Biocca write: "So, if you make a house in virtual reality, and there's another person there in the virtual space with you, you have not created a symbol for a house or a code for a house. You've actually made a house. It's that direct creation of reality; that's what I call post-symbolic communication."[25]

---

24.   Marie-Laure Ryan, *Narrative as Virtual Reality*, p. 59.

Transparency of mind to one another, making a house together—on the one hand, they are attempts to bypass the present boundaries of bodily reality, and to eliminate symbolic reality, in order to attain free-flowing communication and intimacy. To do this in cybernetic abstraction, however, is to lose touch with earthly human existence and the coming of God in the flesh. On the other hand, *efforts to come into unrestricted union point to the deepest longings of the human person.* At the Last Supper, Jesus Christ prayed that His disciples would come into a union so intimate that there would be a mutual indwelling in Divine Persons and in one another. To be made in the image of God is to have the gift of being called into a sharing in divine life. In His Last Discourse, Jesus Christ told those gathered at table with Him: "You must believe me when I say that I am in the Father and the Father is in me; believe it on the evidence of this work, if for no other reason." (Jn. 14:11) He invited them to "Make your home in me, as I make mine in you." (Jn. 15:4)

As Genesis relates, it is not the desire for intensified knowledge and the desire "to have it all" that is the problem—the problem lies in denying basic creatureliness, in attempting to bypass human reality, to grasp independently what can only be realized in truth and love, and can only be fulfilled in eternal life. The cruelest result of such efforts is that a pseudo-form of fulfillment can be perceived as the "real thing." The inner depths of the human person ache for limitless communion and communication, which are the culmination of honest love. Here reside the meanings of personal revelation, personal self-gift, and mutual knowing.

---

25.   Jaron Lanier and Frank Biocca, "An Insider's View of the Future of Virtual Reality," in *Journal of Communications* 42, no. 4 (1992), p. 161, cited by Ryan in *Narrative as Virtual Reality*, pp. 58-59.

There is a desired "transparency" of love, which is expressed in a reflection by Monsignor Luigi Guissani:

> To affirm Christ is to affirm objective beauty that gives us a passion for life and everything becomes transparent to our eyes. It is no coincidence that gladness visible on the face is the main argument for Christian witness in the whole world, before everyone. The gladness of your heart, the older you get, as time passes, is the confirmation to ourselves of what we say and what we believe in. But this gladness emerges, can emerge only from an objective beauty, from something that is objectively beautiful and good. Gladness cannot come from something that is not beautiful or good. In this case you could speak of contentment or satisfaction, but not of gladness.
>
> Christ is the sign with which the mystery coincides, in reality and in history, in the whole universe and in the history of peoples. That is why to affirm Christ is to affirm something objectively beautiful that gives us a passion for life, and everything becomes transparent to our eyes. Because as long as something, a reality, does not become transparent, begin to be transparent, it is like owning it without owning it; its value remains ambivalent.[26]

Note how Guissani interrelates objective reality, beauty, truth, and love and how he points to Christ as the sign with which the mystery coincides "in reality and in history, in the whole universe and in the history of peoples." Genuine transparency of person depends upon those aspects. There is an anecdotal account attributed to President Abraham Lin-

---

26.   Monsignor Luigi Guissani, *Exercises of the Fraternity of Communion and Liberation: The Miracle of Change* (Rimini, 1998), p. 55, as quoted in *Magnificat*, Vol. 4, No. 5 (July, 2002), p. 302.

coln that bears repeating. It is said that after a visitor left his office one day, Lincoln commented to his secretary, "I don't like that man's face." The secretary, somewhat surprised by the remark, replied that no one could help having a given face. Lincoln replied. "Oh, yes, after forty, everyone is responsible for his face." The desire to meet at an interface, to cross into another's mind, exemplified by some who further the potential applications of virtual reality, has a grounding much deeper than technological contrivance. Literally, to cross the interface between persons, divine or human, is the ultimate call of every human being. Heaven is described as seeing God "face to face." This cannot be contrived, "called up" technologically.

Presence and *interface,* directly addressed by those doing research in VR, can prove to be a radical point of theological entry into areas of mutual interest and concern.

4

REAL FOOD AND VIRTUAL NOURISHMENT

S ince simulation and artificiality increasingly characterize the re-fashioning of the human body, it is not surprising that foods which sustain life are likewise being
modified through biotechnical interventions that favor simulation and artificiality. Such interventions have considerable
theological relevance. Before considering this relevance,
however, it is helpful to cite examples of these biotechnical
interventions, together with the reasons for their application
in the world's food supply.

Anomalies abound concerning food and its distribution
in the beginning years of the Third Millennium. In the
United States, televised reports concerning malnourishment
and starvation in disadvantaged nations are punctuated by
advertisements for products that *look* like real foods and
promise the satisfactory taste of real foods while being
mainly simulations. For example, as noted in an earlier chapter, "fat-free-fat" is now being produced. Among other items
that television commercials promote are food products that
prevent the body's retaining any nourishment from them.
Manufacturers of these products promise that what they produce as food and drink will have an appealing taste, and sat-

isfy the appetite, without the body's being able to absorb them as real nourishment. Some products for consumption bear the promise of hunger-prevention, while others suggest that they will alleviate the woes of over-eating.

The advertisers, in responding to consumer desires in terms of their own economic gain, are touching something much deeper: in affluent nations, these commercial inducements both disclose and foster underlying predominant attitudes in the culture concerning food and drink. There is enticing lavishness of display; the offer of instant availability; and the promise of providing maximum pleasure while reducing angst concerning an increase in weight or digestive distress. Such images pervade the cyber milieu and the printed media.

A recent article on the celebration of Thanksgiving in the United States exemplifies the manner in which attitudes toward food have been radically affected by the pervasive tendency to favor what is artificial and simulated, especially in order to prevent an increase in body weight. In a feature essay entitled "The NeoThanksgiving," Renee Schettler described "A Feast with Fewer Carbs than a Slice of Pumpkin Pie." Naming a number of currently popular diet programs, Schettler observed that a "low-carb craze" has become nothing short of a national obsession in the United States, and that it now influences the national observance of Thanksgiving Day, a holiday which originated as a meal of thanksgiving for the foods of the earth, and an expression of peaceful generosity. Schettler conjectured that at least one carb-conscious person at the Thanksgiving table would have "mentally calculated the grand carbohydrate-gram sum before anyone has even said grace."[1] The article gave an estimated sum of carbohydrate grams in a typical Thanksgiving meal—from the gravy thickened with refined flour and cranberries laced with sugar, to "moderately high-glycemic carrots glazed with high-glycemic maple syrup." After glancing over the typical menu for the holiday, the author observed, "How very not-worth-giving-thanks for."[2]

> ...in an attempt to be poundwise, it's all too easy to become carb-foolish. Those in search of low-carb holiday recipe advice from diet books, Atkins e-newsletters, chat rooms, online forums and Google searches can look forward to mashed "potatoes" made from cauliflower, "stuffing" made from crushed pork rinds or "pumpkin pie" made from ricotta cheese blended with pumpkin pie spice and Splenda.[3]

The article ended with advice to a host(ess): should anyone dare to complain that the meal lacked starch, assume a pious smile, and with a slight shake of the head murmur how sad it is when people "lose sight of what the day is all about." While providing suggestions for a menu with sparse carbohydrates, the author, in a tongue-in-cheek commentary, revealed how deeply the attitudes toward food have changed in an affluent society that faces problems of obesity, anorexia and bulimia.

Concomitant with this is a separation between the growing of plants and animals that provide food and the purchasing of pre-packaged foods. The term "fast food" has become a sobriquet for convenience foods in the United States. Often this also means eating in isolation or among strangers who quickly leave a restaurant with their purchase of "fast food." Many people habitually eat while driving to work, watching television, or working at a computer.

---

1.   Renee Schettler, "A Feast with Fewer Carbs Than a Slice of Pumpkin Pie," in *The Washington Post* (November 19, 2003), p. F1.

2.   Schettler, "A Feast with Fewer Carbs," p. F1.

3.   Schettler, "A Feast with Fewer Carbs," p. F9.

A radio commercial aired for a restaurant in the United States' capitol appeals to those who (even subconsciously) may perceive that the eating of food can have a greater meaning. The restaurant invites prospective clients to experience a "European style" of dining. Utilizing a foreign accent, the advertiser says: "You Americans say 'Let's do lunch' or 'Let's grab a bite to eat.' What's this 'doing and grabbing'?" He then invites future customers to experience an unhurried meal. In an atmosphere where food is hastily eaten, even "grabbed" as a timesaving device, and where the contents of a meal are "not what they seem," the gift of eating is radically diminished. Contemporary lifestyles provide an entry point for what can be called "reductionist" intake of food.

Fascination with speed and convenience in the production of food products is not a recent contrivance. Already in the 1960's Alan Watts offered a scathing description of the mass production of bread:

> To begin with, the wheat is grown, unloved, by industrial farming over millions of featureless and treeless acres in such wastelands as Kansas and Nebraska, and is sprayed by airplane with Flit and Bugdeath. It is then shaved off the face of the earth with immense mechanical clippers, winnowed, and ground into a flour which, by washing with detergents and stewing in disinfectants, is converted into tons of pancake makeup. In vast automated baking factories these mountains of pure chalk-dust are mixed with pantothenic acid, pyridoxine, para-aminobenzoic acid, and artificial flavorings, whereafter the whole mass is bubbleized, stabilized by heating, sliced, wrapped in wax paper, and shipped out in the form of sleazy cushions which are unfortunately too small and too perishable to be used as bolsters.[4]

As noted earlier, genuine humor is based on the familiar. Food, and the anomalies connected with its consumption, are frequently the grist for cartoonists. Recently, the syndicated cartoon "Baby Blues" featured a mother-child dialogue at mealtime. The child, looking at the food on her plate, asks what it is. When the mother assures her that it is *beef*, the child eats and tells her mother: "That's good; just so it isn't cow. I like cows." The separation between eating within a relational context, and personal participation in the growing and preparation of food products, can lead to indifference regarding its reality. In an article called "Will Frankenfood Feed the World?" Bill Gates pointed out that by the year 2000, genetically modified foods were "already very much a part of our lives," and that one-third of the corn and more than half of cotton and soybeans grown in the United States "were the product of biotechnology, according to the Department of Agriculture."[5]

N. Katherine Hayles has recognized the direct connection between technical approaches to the human body and issues regarding the eating of food. She notes that in the *posthuman* viewpoint, there are "no essential differences or absolute demarcations between bodily existence and computer simulation, cybernetic mechanism and biological organism, robot technology and human goals."[6] When the human being is perceived as a set of informational processes, the body is not essential; indeed, it can be "erased." In this viewpoint, there is also an erasure of the markers of bodily differences, such as race, sex, and ethnicity. Hayles relates this to eating, citing the study of Gillian Brown which shows a con-

---

4.   Alan Watts. *Does It Matter? Essays on Man's Relation to Materiality* (New York, 1970), p. 30.

5.   See Bill Gates, "Will Frankenfood Feed the World?" in *Time*, 155, 25 (June 19, 2000), p. 78.

6.   N. Katherine Hayles, *How We Became Posthuman, p. 3.*

nection between humanism and anorexia. Brown's study
indicates that:

> ...the anorexic's struggle to "decrement" the body is
> possible precisely because the body is understood as an
> object for control and mastery rather than as an intrinsic
> part of the self. Quoting an anorectic's remark—"You
> make out of your body your very own kingdom where
> you are the tyrant, the absolute dictator"—Brown states,
> "Anorexia is thus a fight for self-control, a flight from the
> slavery food threatens; self-sustaining, self-possession
> independent of bodily desires is the anorectic's crucial
> goal." ...the anorectic creates a physical image that, in its
> skeletal emaciation, serves as material testimony that the
> locus of the liberal humanist subject lies in the mind, not
> the body.... William Gibson makes the point vividly in
> *Neuromancer* when the narrator characterizes the posthu-
> man body as "data made flesh."[7]

The prevalence of eating disorders exemplifies one
dimension of the ambiguity concerning food, experienced
among peoples in the affluent countries of the West. An
information bulletin, prepared for the Governor's Drug-Free
Communities Grants Program is entitled "Eating Disorders:
Obesity, Bulimia, and Anorexia, A Cultural Epidemic."[8] A
statistic from the report shows the severity of the problem.
The opening sentences state: "In a recent survey, 80 per cent
of 11-year-old girls said they feel overweight and are dieting.
Eating disorders are most likely to occur among young people, and both boys and girls are susceptible." Eating disorders are usually associated with secrecy, the report states, and
ending this secrecy is usually the first step toward recovery.
Even then, it takes time to recover. It may take people two or

---

7.   N. Katherine Hayles, *How We Became Posthuman*, p. 5.

three years to develop a new relationship with food, themselves and others, according to the report.

The production of artificial and simulated food products, the increasing technical interventions in the growing and manufacturing of foods, and the prevalence of eating disorders mark Western cultures at the beginning of the Third Christian Millennium and raise theological questions closely associated with the realm of the virtual.

WHY SHOULD THESE MATTERS CONCERN THEOLOGIANS?

From the opening chapters of Genesis to the Book of Revelation, the provision of food and the eating of food are predominant themes that express the divine-human relationship and the Mystery of Salvation. Although the *genre* of writing employed in Genesis II-III is not intended to express historical data, the basic truth concerning the fall of humanity in foundational origins is conveyed in terms of eating forbidden fruit—a deliberate choice that represented

---

8.   See http://www.naples.net/social/jft0001.htm regarding the preparation of this report. Further information is available from Florida Alcohol and Drug Abuse Association, 1030 E. Lafayette Street, Suite 100, Tallahassee, FL 32301 904-878-2196. The report describes major eating disorders: "Obesity, bulimia, and anorexia nervosa are three types of eating disorders. People try to hide an eating disorder, often by bingeing, bingeing and purging, or starving. Bingeing is out-of-control eating often thousands of calories at a time with or without pleasure. Obesity, a medical problem in its own right, can result from bingeing and poor food choices. Bulimics binge and then purge (get rid of food by vomiting, taking laxatives, or exercising excessively). Anorexics starve themselves, sometimes to the point of death," p.1.

independence from God and an act which defied creatureliness and limitation. The Book of Revelation, the culminating work of the Christian Canon of Scripture, also anticipates the meaning of eternal life in complementary imagery: "If anyone has ears to hear, let him listen to what the Spirit is saying to the churches: those who prove victorious I will feed *from the tree of life set in* God's *paradise.*" (Rev. 2:7) and "...to those who prove victorious I will give the hidden manna and a white stone—a stone with *a new name* written on it, known only to the man who receives it." (Rev. 2:17)

The imagery of fruitful gardens and heavenly-supplied manna, present in the opening and closing books, recurs in numerous places in Scripture and marks the significance of eating and drinking. Abraham is given the opportunity not only to sacrifice animals in preparation for cutting covenant with God, but also to provide a meal for Yahweh from his own herd and provisions. "Yahweh appeared to him at the Oak of Mamre while he was sitting by the entrance of the tent during the hottest part of the day. He looked up, and there he saw three men standing near him. As soon as he saw them he ran from the entrance of the tent to meet them, and bowed to the ground. 'My lord,' he said, 'I beg you, if I find favour with you, kindly do not pass your servant by. A little water shall be brought; you shall wash your feet and lie down under the tree. Let me fetch a little bread and you shall refresh yourselves before going further. That is why you have come in your servant's direction.'" (Gen. 18:1-5) He tells Sarah to hurry in kneading loaves of bread while he runs to the herd, chooses a fine calf and directs his servant to prepare it in haste. He serves the guests, who then reveal to him and his wife Sarah that they will conceive a child—a human impossibility at their age, but a singular possibility with God. "Is anything too wonderful for Yahweh?" Abraham is asked.

Throughout the Old and New Testaments, it is evident that divine Revelation is frequently given in the context of a meal. When the Israelites are to be freed from slavery in Egypt, it is the sacrificial meal that marks the occasion. That meal, specified in liturgical detail, was the effective sign of deliverance not only for those leaving for the Promised Land, but for all who would enter into the renewal of the covenant with God, a renewal celebrated yearly at the Seder meal. When the Israelites in the desert wailed for food and drink, God provided manna, quail, and water. During his desert sojourn, the prophet Elijah was sustained by divinely provided food.

It is Jesus Christ, however, who brings the meaning of food and drink to fullest realization. Following His baptism by John in the Jordan, Jesus was led by the Spirit to go into the wilderness where He would be tempted by the devil. The tempter approached Jesus, first of all, in terms of food. "If you are the Son of God, tell these stones to turn into loaves." (Mt. 4:3) The response of Jesus has particular relevance in our present struggles with food and its production. He assured the devil, "Man does not live on bread alone but on every word that comes from the mouth of God." (Mt. 4:4)

In that cogent rejection of turning stones into bread, Jesus engaged several levels concerning bread, its meaning and availability. Beyond spurning suggestion from the evil spirit, Jesus made it clear that bread is not simply a commodity; rather, it relates to receiving the divine Word. This would be realized beyond any human power to imagine in the Eucharist. Second, speedy self-convenience was not the measure for producing bread. He would later provide bread for those fainting with hunger, not from stones, but from within the already existent potential of bread itself.

How poignant, then, are the questions of Jesus: "What father among you would hand his son a stone when he asked for bread? Or hand him a snake instead of a fish? Or hand

him a scorpion if he asked for an egg?" (Lk. 11:11-12)
Thirdly, although the devil rightly understood that Jesus had
the *power* to change stones into bread, the Lord rejected such
a change. Simply having the power to effect a radical change
in the nature of beings does not mean that it should be done.
Stone has a goodness and reality in itself, as does bread. Jesus
did not *equate* the two or effect an exchange between them
arbitrarily in order to show his ability to utilize extraordinary
powers or to satisfy an immediate personal need. Rather, He
would later show the remarkable potential already present in
the simple realities of everyday life: water, wheat, grapes and
fish.

Jesus' great respect for food and drink was an enduring
mark of His public ministry. His mother called Him into
His public mission by evoking the first of His "signs" at the
wedding feast of Cana. In what no one could have anticipated, He showed the marvelous potential already inherent
in water destined to become wine. He did not disdain the
need for food and drink. With keen sensitivity, upon raising
the daughter of Jairus, Jesus did not tell the parents to have
her formulate a prayer of thanks. Rather, He told them to
give the child something to eat. When the crowds who had
come to hear His teaching had no food and would become
faint on their journey home, He showed concern and multiplied the small amount of bread and fish at hand in order to
satisfy their hunger. All of this was leading to the *ultimate*
potential of bread.

It was in the context of meals that He taught the meaning of forgiveness, the supremacy of love, and the dignity of
service. Jesus invited Zacchaeus to descend from the
sycamore tree because He "must come to his house" that very
day. He was inviting himself to Zacchaeus's home, his center
of hospitality, simultaneously provoking the taxman's con-
version. The home of Martha, Mary and Lazarus was certainly a focus of meals, as indicated by the dialogue

concerning Martha's anxiety over food preparation, and by the banquet held there a week after Lazarus had been restored to life. It was at a Samaritan well that Jesus initiated His revelatory message to the woman of many husbands by asking her for a drink of water, and then speaking of Himself as the source of living water that would satisfy thirst forever.

Food was also a frequent theme in the parables of Jesus. When the prodigal son returns to his father, asking forgiveness for his wanton way of life and offering to be a servant, the father asks for robe and ring, and tells the servants to prepare a great feast. Rejection by the leaders of his own people led Jesus to propose the parable of the king who prepared a great feast and invited many. When those invited found excuses for non-attendance, the king sent out his servants to compel those in the "byways" to come and fill the banquet hall. For the guest who came to the wedding feast without wearing the proper garment, however, there was severe punishment. There is an appropriate way to come to a Feast, emphasizing the dignity of both the persons invited and the nature of what it means to "eat together."

There is a poignant saying in Jesus' parable about servants who were prepared for their master's return from the wedding feast. Luke's Gospel has Jesus say, "Happy those servants whom the master finds awake when he comes. I tell you solemnly, he will put on an apron, sit them down at table and wait on them." (Lk. 12:37) Everyday experiences of need for food find their way into the parables, such as the man who knocks on the door in the middle of the night to ask bread for unexpected guests and the child who asks his father for a fish. Jesus compared the kingdom of God to a woman burying yeast in the flour so that the whole bread be leavened.

The Gospel of John, in very concrete terms, reveals the meaning and deep intercommunion among real food, real body and real symbol. The sixth chapter of this Gospel opens with Jesus having gone "to the other side of the Sea of Galilee." Seeing the crowds approaching, He asked Philip where they might buy bread for the people to eat although "He himself knew exactly what He was going to do." Taking five barley loaves and two fish, He gave thanks and then distributed food, enough for all, with twelve baskets of fragments left over. This was the decisive occasion that opened to a revelation that none of His followers could have anticipated. The day after the feeding of the multitude, when the crowds found Him and the disciples on the "other side of the lake," Jesus told them "most solemnly" that the reason they followed Him was not because of "...the signs but because you had all the bread you wanted to eat." He told them that it wasn't Moses who gave their ancestors manna in the desert, but His Father. Now, however, they were to receive a still greater gift, because the Father was giving them "the bread from heaven, the true bread." Jesus identified Himself in terms of this food from heaven: "I am the bread of life. He who comes to me will never be hungry; he who believes in me will never thirst." (Jn. 6: 35) When the crowd began to complain about His teaching, Jesus revealed to them:

> I am the living bread which has come down from heaven.
> Anyone who eats this bread will live forever;
> and the bread that I shall give
> is my flesh, for the life of the world. (Jn. 6: 51)

This made the crowds argue: how can this man give us his own flesh to eat? Jesus continued:

> I tell you most solemnly,
> if you do not eat the flesh of the Son of Man
> and drink his blood,
> you will not have life in you.
> Anyone who does eat my flesh and drink my blood
> has eternal life,

and I shall raise him up on the last day.
For my flesh is real food
and my blood is real drink.
He who eats my flesh and drinks my blood
lives in me
and I live in him. (Jn. 6: 53-56) *[author's italics]*

It was the moment of decision, given in the graphic terms of bread, of body and blood to be received and eaten. Most of the crowd left Jesus at that point. Turning to the Twelve, Jesus asked them to choose: "What about you, do you want to go away too?" Peter spoke for the Twelve: "Lord, who shall we go to? You have the message of eternal life, and we believe; we know that you are the Holy One of God." (Jn. 6: 68-69)

At the Last Supper Jesus fulfilled the promise of self-gift in His body and blood given as food and drink. It was the transformation of the Paschal Meal, bringing to fullness what had been prefigured in the Passover Meal in Egypt, the manna in the desert and all of the Paschal Seders celebrated through the centuries. It brought into vivid meaning the sacredness of *every* meal that He had eaten at Nazareth, Bethany and Capharnaum.

The enduring significance of Jesus Christ's self-gift as food and drink has been realized perpetually in the resurrection. On the day of resurrection, Jesus joined two of His disheartened followers on their way to Emmaus, and accepted their invitation to stay with them. While they were at table, He took bread, blessed it, broke it and gave it to them. It was then that "their eyes were opened and they recognized him." (Lk. 24: 31) It was through food that Jesus confirmed His authentic presence to the incredulous Apostles who were fearfully gathered behind locked doors in the upper room. After inviting them to look upon His hands and feet and to realize that "a ghost has no flesh and bones as you can see I have," He asked if they had anything to eat: "And they offered him a piece of grilled fish, which he took and ate before their eyes." (Lk. 24: 43)

When Peter and his companions returned to Galilee and took up the familiar ritual of fishing in the Sea of Galilee, they labored all night without a catch. It was the Risen Christ who not only filled their nets with fish, but invited them to a breakfast that He had prepared on the shore, encouraging them to bring "some of the fish you have just caught" (Jn. 21:10) to contribute to the breakfast. That meal would culminate in the confirmation of Peter's commission to assume the founding leadership of the Church: to *feed* both lambs and sheep. Once again, the enduring Presence of the Risen Christ was manifested in the intimacy of eating together, and the provision of food for others.

In these foundational experiences of revelation and faith, the theological issues of the present time find a crucial point of reference. The profound issues regarding the growing of food products, their preparation and eating, have a basis not only in human identity and the meaning of created realities—they pertain, above all, to the Person of Christ who is forever given as food and drink in the Eucharist. He has identified himself as living bread, as *real food and real drink*.

It is of deep concern, then, that the majority of people in some nations are starving while people in affluent nations eat products that simulate real foods while attempting to circumvent the nutrition that real food could provide. Likewise, it is of concern that many people eat in isolation, great haste, sometimes not even paying attention to the kind of food they are consuming. Some food products are advertised in ways that make the food itself seem to bear an aspect of evil, something to be avoided. It is commonplace for manufacturers to name food products in ways that entice the eater while suggesting guilt. For example, some foods bear labels that describe them as "temptation" or "sinfully delicious."

There is great significance in the attitudes toward food and eating that are manifested by the manner in which foods are grown, produced, and presented to be eaten.

Of particular theological concern are 1) the artificiality of many food products; 2) the attempts to negate authentic nourishment from the eating of food; 3) the genetic alteration of plants and animals in ways that irreversibly change their composition; and 4) the association of eating and drinking with guilt and evil. Each of these has elements of the virtual which impact the understanding of Eucharist and interpersonal communion within the Church.

First, then, the artificiality of many food products has a great bearing on understanding the Eucharist. To hold and correctly clarify the meaning of the Eucharist is a core aspect of Catholic faith, and thus the deepened understanding of it is a matter of enduring theological concern. It is belief in the authentic presence of Jesus Christ in the Eucharist through the appearance of bread and wine that brought the Second Vatican Council to express so cogently the Most Sacred Mystery of the Eucharist in *The Constitution on the Sacred Liturgy:* "a sacrament of love, a sign of unity, a bond of charity, a paschal banquet in which Christ is consumed, the mind is filled with grace, and a pledge of future glory is given to us."[9] The faithful, the document says, are to be conscious of what they are doing and "be nourished at the table of the Lord's Body."[10]

Likewise, the *Catechism of the Catholic Church* cites Article #11 of *Lumen Gentium*, the Dogmatic Constitution on the Church, which calls the Eucharist "the source and summit of the Christian life."[11] The entire catechesis on the

---

9.   *The Constitution on the Sacred Liturgy,* #47.
10.   *The Constitution on the Sacred Liturgy,* #48.
11.   *Catechism of the Catholic Church,* #1324.

Eucharist given in the *Catechism* emphasizes the sacred reality of Christ's presence, true body and blood. In explicating the phrase applied to the Eucharist as the "breaking of bread," paragraph #1329 states that it is called:

> The *Breaking of Bread,* because Jesus used this rite, part of a Jewish meal, when as master of the table he blessed and distributed the bread, above all at the Last Supper. It is by this action that his disciples will recognize him after his Resurrection, and it is this expression that the first Christians will use to designate their Eucharistic assemblies; by doing so they signified that all who eat the one broken bread, Christ, enter into communion with him and form but one body in him.

The Eucharist is also called "the holy things," "the bread of angels," "the bread from heaven," "the medicine of immortality," and *viaticum,* as noted in #1331 of the *Catechism.*

It was in the context of a sacred meal that Jesus washed the feet of His Apostles and gave His commandment of love. "In order to leave them a pledge of this love, in order never to depart from His own and to make them sharers in His Passover, He instituted the Eucharist as the memorial of His death and Resurrection, and commanded His apostles to celebrate it until His return." (#1337) How important it is for faith and theological reflection to realize the goodness, the sacredness and the *authenticity* of the Eucharist as real food and drink, as real Body and Blood of the Lord.

In a milieu abounding with artificial food products (and many, while eating, attempting to eliminate the nourishment derived from them) it will become increasingly difficult to maintain the understanding of Eucharist in its authentic reality and meaning. Recent polls conducted in the United States indicate that many practicing Catholics do not believe in the Real Presence of Christ in the Eucharist. The central-ity of this truth of faith will then be diminished, or even seem of little importance to them as they receive Holy Communion. The passionate affirmation of the truth of Eucharist to the point of martyrdom—characteristic of the early Church—is sometimes supplanted today by a polite casualness in the receiving of Communion. Receiving the profound Mystery of Christ's Presence can become perfunctory, reduced to a community ritual of remembrance, a gesture of fellowship that is open to personal interpretation. If there is no realization of the personal presence of Christ, Body and Blood, soul and divinity in the Eucharist—that is, if the reception of the sacrament is understood as participating in fellowship through a sharing of small rounds of bread and a goblet of wine—then, it can seem an affront to persons not of the Catholic faith to deprive them of such fellowship.

Pope John Paul II, in his encyclical letter *Ecclesia de Eucharistia,* describes the Eucharist as the pledge of bodily resurrection at the end of the world. Moreover, he writes, that those who "feed on Christ" already receive eternal life. "With the Eucharist we digest, as it were, the 'secret' of the resurrection."[12] This is in continuity, however, with the sacrificial aspect of the Eucharist. The Pope points out that there is a *causal* influence in the Eucharist. In offering Himself to the Apostles as food and drink, Jesus was mysteriously involving them in the sacrifice to be completed on Calvary. This would not simply be a figurative expression, as Jesus had clarified earlier. At a heady moment when Jesus seemed to be in ascendancy of power, James and John asked the favor of being seated at His right and left "in your glory." Jesus assures them that they do not know what they are asking, and then places the question to them: "Can you drink

---

12.   Pope John Paul II, *Ecclesia de Eucharistia* (St. Peter's, Rome, April 17, 2003), #18.

the cup that I must drink, or be baptized with the baptism with which I must be baptized?" (Mk. 10:38) The *reality* of eating and drinking with and of Christ became watershed moments not only for the eager brothers, but for the thousands who had been fed by miraculously multiplied bread and for all who would profess Eucharistic faith. Belief in the Real Presence of Christ in the Eucharist remains decisive in the present time, and this resonates throughout daily life.

Attitudes toward food and drink not only affect the rituals experienced in family and community life, but undergird understandings of sacramental life, either positively or negatively. Thus, what is simulated, artificial, or *virtually* experienced within a culture, or within family life, is of concern not only for systematic theology, but for liturgical and pastoral theology.

Two simple items may exemplify this. The first involves the wedding cake shared with guests at the wedding reception. It is a familiar ritual for a newly married couple to place their hands together on the knife that cuts the first piece of the wedding cake. Then, after cutting the first piece together—in a gesture that has deep meaning for those who truly understand what they are enacting—the spouses simultaneously feed one another with that first piece of cake. Regrettably, this has degenerated in some cases so that some couples, in jest, literally shove the pieces of cake into one another's face. The meaning of the ritual is not only lost but also reduced to an indignity. The capacity to understand the beauty of the ritual depends upon the meaning that each of the partners has internalized regarding food, its preparation and presentation, and the sacredness of mutual nourishing of one another as spouses. How few there are who might relate this ritual to *The Song of Songs*, to the marriage vows just spoken, and to Eucharistic self-gift in the Body and the Blood received as food.

A second example concerns the ritual of family meals. As noted above, from Cana to the Last Supper, the most central revelations of Jesus were given in the context of meals. It is difficult for persons who have not experienced the simple, consistent ritual of family meals to know the significance of Jesus' revelations and actions being integrated within meals. Recently, the mother of a family related an occurrence in their home that underscored the value of family meals. There are seven children in the family, and both parents are employed outside the home. Yet the family consistently eats the evening meal together. Recently, two boys, friends of a teen-age member of the family, were present when it was time for the evening meal. The mother invited them to stay. After momentary hesitation, they joined the family at table. The mother noted that the two guests were rather perplexed, and finally one said, "You mean you do this every day?" He was stunned that it was not only possible for a family to come together for a daily supper, but also that this was part of a way of life that he had never known.

Father Raymond Ellis, pastor of St. Cecelia's Church in the inner city of Detroit during the 1960's and early 1970's, realized the significance of linking the Eucharist with all of life. In those tumultuous years in Detroit, when the inner city was erupting with frustration over wretched living conditions and prejudice, Father Ellis knew that sacramental life could not touch the depths of people's lives without simultaneously touching familial roots, relationships, and the manner in which daily life extended into the community. In a certain sense, he initiated the difficult process of reconciliation and healing by teaching a reverence for food. Hiring young men for work in the large complex of parish buildings, he started "at the bottom of the food chain" with garbage. Seeing how the alleys of the inner city were rank with raw garbage, he began to relate the meaning of food and its remains with Philippians Chapter 2, where Paul describes

Jesus Christ's emptying himself on our behalf. Ellis worked sided-by-side with those employed, telling them that the grapefruit rinds and coffee grounds were also "poured out" for us. The way to respect that, he said, was "to give them a decent burial." He became known as the priest with "a theology of garbage." He invited parishioners to come one night a week to "Contemporize the Gospel" that would be read on the following Sunday. He would draw upon insights gained at those meetings in preparing his Sunday homilies.

One evening Father Ellis came late for the meeting that dealt with the sixth chapter of John's Gospel on the promise of the Eucharist. He slumped in his chair and said that he could not preach on that passage the following Sunday and then explained why. He had hired a young man to clean floors in the parish school and, working side-by-side, taught him how to use the machines for washing, waxing, and buffing. He went to assist others and upon returning, found that the young man, despite clear instruction, had not washed the floor, but simply waxed over the dirt. Once more he taught the process, left, and returned later only to find that, again, fresh wax covered a soiled floor. Ellis told of getting angry and ordering the young man to leave. He said simply "I cannot stomach that young man. Until I can stomach him I cannot preach on eating the body and blood of Christ." Despite parishioners' telling him that his anger was honest, in his Sunday homily he related to the parish what had happened and his experience of inability to speak directly of John 6 regarding the Eucharistic promise.

When Father Ellis spoke to young children preparing for First Communion, he would earnestly tell them, to their astonishment: "I am going to eat you," explaining how closely his own reception of Eucharist was linked to them and their daily lives. Apart from an intense conviction of the Eucharist as "real food and drink," such teaching would be without meaning. Ellis died from a heart attack when he was only in his early forties, having himself poured out life unstintingly for others. It was a maxim of his to say that the problem of racism is not a general one, of trying to get people to love those of another race. The crux of the difficulty, he said, is that of truly being able to love ONE authentically. Being able to love *one* authentically, with all of the relationships, extensions, and depths that such love involves, necessarily means openness to loving all, he explained. He would say by way of contemporary parable—if I say that I love peanuts, I don't have to eat every peanut. *How* I eat ONE will show whether I love peanuts.

There is a profound interrelationship among all truths. This calls for a deepening authenticity in living such simple realities as eating and drinking. Thomas Merton began his *Thoughts on Solitude*:

> There is no greater disaster in the spiritual life than to be immersed in unreality, for life is maintained and nourished in us by our vital relation with realities outside and above us.
>
> When our life feeds on unreality, it must starve. It must therefore die. There is no greater misery than to mistake this fruitless death for the true, fruitful and sacrificial "death" by which we enter into life.
>
> The death by which we enter into life is not an escape from reality, but a complete gift of ourselves which involves a total commitment to reality.[13]

The "Our Father" is very spare, but it contains the petition, "Give us this day our daily bread." The request resonates with the anticipation of eternal life as a "Heavenly

---

13.   Thomas Merton, *Thoughts in Solitude* (Boston, 1993), p. 3.

Banquet," the Wedding Feast. It is important to emphasize once again Jesus' saying "...my flesh is real food and my blood is real drink." (Jn. 6:55) No marital act bears the same intimacy as that of receiving another as *real* food and drink. Jesus promised the capacity of his living within those who would receive him, and in turn, the human capacity to live within him. It is at this depth that theology must grapple with the issues of the virtual, the simulated, and the artificial regarding food and drink.

5

FREEDOM, TRUTH, SEXUALITY:
AT THE INTERFACE

*K*en Hillis makes a helpful distinction between the acronyms *VR* (virtual reality) and *VE* (virtual environment). He makes this distinction, he writes, because *virtual reality* is a hybrid term that refers to individual experiences, constituted technologically, that are able "to represent nature, with the broad and overlapping spheres of social relations and meaning." By way of distinction, then, Hillis describes "VE's [virtual environments] to be representational spaces that propose particular spatial illusions or fantasies."[1] In *VR*, there is an assumption that a series of existing social relations "based on an individualistic understanding and practice of pluralism might be relocated to a disembodied datascape—an immaterial landscape 'wherein' military exercises, commercial transactions, virtual 'on-the-job training,' and so on increasingly 'take place.'"[2] Two assumptions are made here, says Hillis. The first assumption

---

1.   Ken Hillis, *Digital Sensations* (Minneapolis, 1999), p. xv.
2.   Ibid.

is that relocating what is *concrete* to an imaginary or "meta-phoric space" makes an act of communication a completely adequate "substitute for embodied experiential reality; it exchanges communications technologies for the reality of places and dispenses with, for example, empiricism's concerns about sense data and how things are understood as true and/or real."[3] A second assumption is that "as mere automata, our animalistic and all too finite physical bodies are thought secondary to our minds and representational forms—a dynamic that is built into virtual technologies."[4] To varying degrees, says Hillis, all cultures attempt to facilitate the escape from the body, its needs and actions in regard to food, sex, and death. The attempt to escape can bring about a denial of embodied reality and its constraints.

Hillis cites the nineteenth century American trek to the West as an escapist movement in *real space*—many hoping to find Utopia and to leave history behind. Now that "Route 66" is no longer available as an escape passage, the "information superhighways" allow users to migrate to "electronic frontiers." They offer alternatives to a physical taking-to-the-road. In this way, technology seems to offer an alternative to the natural world, with virtual realities freeing the imagination from having to deal with mundane realities (which are already modified by technology).

Both *virtual reality* (described by Hillis as individual experiences which represent nature and have overlapping spheres of social relation and meaning) and *virtual environment* (specified as representational spaces that propose particular spatial illusions or fantasies) have theological implications in regard to human freedom, truth, and human identity.

---

3.   Ibid.
4.   *Digital Sensations,* pp. xv and xvi.

IMMERSIVE VIRTUAL TECHNOLOGY

In particular, it is the virtual aspects of *immersion* and *network communication* that need to be considered as impacting the meaning of truth, human freedom, and personal identity. *Immersion,* as the term is employed here, refers to the electronically facilitated merger of human and machine. Hillis says: "Immersive virtual technology...radically shrinks, if not eliminates, the actual distance between the user's eyes and the HMD [head monitoring device] screen to less than an inch.... [It] involves the technology's ability to facilitate the adoption, trying on, or acting out of multiple aspects of the self."[5] For some decades it was postulated that eventually it would be possible to effect cyborgs: the union of human and machine. To a certain extent this is happening, as the interface between human persons and technical devices becomes a porous border, a two-way passage of mutual influence, choice and action.

This interconnection between the human person and technical apparatus is different from the singularly human act of reading a work of fiction, viewing a film in a theater, or even participating in a dramatic presentation or historical reenactment. The latter kinds of interaction involve some impact on the one who views a performance, or physically participates in the work, but this is basically different from

---

5. *Digital Sensations*, p. 164. He adds: "VR offers conceptual access to a space perhaps best appreciated by people manifesting multiple personalities, and who, by their interest in VR, are responding to cultural demands that fracture identities previously held to be more unified (Stone 1992b). VR can be seen to support the fragmentation of identity and render proliferating individual subidentities and their experiences into commodity form. A VE also provides a space of performance, a multipurpose theater-in-the-round for the many components of the self," p. 164.

the technical/human interchange that happens in virtual reality and the cyber-space known as *VE*. Garrison Keillor's fictional *Lake Wobegon,* for example, continues to attract radio listeners and theater-goers who observe the production of the broadcast, not because it fosters escape from daily life, but rather because the characters, episodes, and descriptions of small-town life in twentieth century Minnesota *express the realities of ordinary life,* allowing familiar identification with the characters and situation, and even have the potential to evoke greater self-understanding.[6] Like Flannery O'Connor, who used her imaginative genius as a writer of short stories to portray the deeply human elements of ordinary life in American mid-twentieth century Georgia, Garrison Keillor writes with an appreciation of relationships, suffering, and the joys and sorrows that include acceptance of limitations in self and others. He also perceives the manner in which the extended non-human environment participates in real events: "One farmer told me that barns start falling apart if the cattle are evacuated; cows keep the temperature and humidity up, and if they are sold off, the barn goes to pieces fairly quickly. A symbiotic relationship."[7] What may seem very elemental in this example has a meaningful bearing here. It concerns the use of human experience, observation, imagination and innovative creativity *in relation to what is*

---

6.   See "In Search of Lake Wobegon," in *National Geographic* (December, 2000), p. 90. Keillor writes that when he invented the town of Lake Wobegon close to thirty years ago, people would ask if it *is* a real town, and where it is located. "I used to say it's fiction. 'Oh,' they said, 'Sure.' But they were disappointed. People want stories to be true. They don't care so much about your gifts of invention as the fact that your story reminded them of people they knew when growing up."

7.   Keillor, "In Search of Lake Wobegon," p. 95.

authentic and relational, in a manner that can lead to insight and relational development.

How does *VE* differ from this? Hillis gives a description by Margaret Morse:

> Travelers on...virtual highways...have...at least one body too many—the one now largely sedentary carbon-based body at the control console that suffers hunger, corpulency, illness, old age, and ultimately death. The other body, a silicon-based surrogate jacked into immaterial realms of data, has superpowers, albeit virtually, and is immortal—or, rather, the chosen body, an electronic avatar "decoupled" from the physical body, is a program capable of enduring endless deaths.[8]

Hillis recalls having received a final call for papers on "The Body" to be presented in the 1998 Annual Conference of British Geographers, sponsored by the Social and Cultural Geography and the Population Geography Research Groups. He said that the call for papers used a "hook" to attract prospective presenters. The announcement questioned: "The Body: Is the body dead? Has it been 'done'?" Hillis noted that beyond the purpose of attracting interest, the phrases used suggested that "'the body' is already a shopworn, threadbare commodity, ready to be recycled, while 'cutting-edge' academics move on to better and more 'marginal' areas of inquiry than the now outmoded and therefore soon to be 'discarded body.'"[9] In reality, the body is not only the out-

---

8.   Hillis, *Digital Sensations,* p. 166. See also Margaret Morse, "What Do Cyborgs Eat? Oral Logic in an Information Society," in Gretchen Bender and Timothy Druckrey ed. *Culture on the Brink: Ideologies of Technology,* Dia Center for the Arts, no. 9 (Seattle: Bay Press, 1994).
9.   *Digital Sensations,* p. 168.

ward, integral manifestation of the whole person. The human body, as outward expression of the person, locates the person, gives the entire person a place and presence in the universe. The body in its uniqueness manifests a specific appearance, a certain physique, voice, and manner of gesturing that identify the person, making them recognizable, available. It is in and through the lived body that the deepest aspects of person are relationally expressed.[10]

In "virtual environment," however, the person who is bonded with technical materials, projects an avatar (or a variety of avatars) of the self into a virtual space—projected configurations that can change and be changed in the interactivity of human and machine. A fragmentation takes place in which the projection is mainly a function of *seeing* what is fabricated. *VE* depends mainly on sight. An illustration by Liz McKenzie sketches the fragmentation of identity that occurs in virtual space. Several perceptions of self are going on, as it were. On the user side of the interface there is already a sense of "seeing oneself" while as many as four different "virtual selves" or avatars within the virtual space either gaze back on the real body as a "shell" or at one

---

10.   In *Body Theology: God's Presence in Man's World* (New York, 1973), Arthur Vogel wrote: "The body we live is the means of our basic orientation to reality. Bodily defects, just like bodily abilities, are primary factors in organizing the worlds in which we immediately live.... The body we live is not something to which we must give meaning before it is significant to us; it is meaningful to us in the first instance, and becomes a source of the meaning of other things because it is the primary location of our presence. The body gives location to presence.... Personal presence is more than the body, but we are able to know it to be more through the body and never without a body. Human presence needs the body in order to be itself, for body-meaning anchors us in the world," pp. 89, 91.

another *as* other. If the user of *VE* is trying to escape alienation, he may find that within *VE*'s, alienation proliferates. Hillis explains that "the fracture of self-identity implicit in the relationship 'I see myself' is seemingly multiplied in 'I see *Me* seeing myself seeing myself'; and this fracture gains support within a cultural context expressed by the phrase 'I like to watch.'"[11]

There are further proliferations of "watching" made possible by the developing technologies. While the users of virtual reality can experience multiple points of view, they are also subject to being watched. Hayles maintains that the stylized gestures of the hand used in *VR* simulation bring about changes in the configuration of the user's brain, some of which are long lasting. While humans build computers, they are being molded by them.[12]

VIRTUAL IMMERSION AND FREEDOM

It is evident that interaction of persons with virtual spaces, avatars, and scenarios involves human freedom. "Freedom" is a universal term ranging across widely differing descriptions and interpretations. For some, freedom means the absence of all external constraints. For others, it means the capacity *to will* what is to be done and the uninhibited capacity to carry out what has been willed. Currently, the word "choice" has increasingly come to mean the latter. Advocates of uninhibited choice defend it as a basic legal "right" accorded to every individual. A third broad way of understanding freedom involves the recognition that acts of

---

11.   *Digital Sensations*, pp. 107-108.
12.   N. Katherine Hayles, "Virtual Bodies and Flickering Images," in *October*, 66 (fall), cited in *Digital Sensations*, p. 111.

choosing and willing not only express personal decision and relationship, but also include responsibility to persons and laws which are external to the individual, whether these be religious or civic in nature.

The *Catechism of the Catholic Church* characterizes human freedom as "the power, rooted in reason and will, to act or not to act, to do this or that, and so to perform deliberate actions on one's own responsibility.... Human freedom is a force for growth and maturity in truth and goodness; it attains its perfection when directed toward God, our beatitude. As long as freedom has not bound itself definitively to its ultimate good which is God, there is the possibility of *choosing between good and evil*, and thus of growing in perfection or of failing and sinning."[13] The *Catechism* asserts that human persons are responsible for their voluntary actions and that the will's mastery over acts is enhanced by asceticism, the practice of virtue, and growth in knowledge of the good. Human persons have the inalienable right to the exercise of their freedom, especially in moral and religious matters, and this right is to be recognized and protected by civil authority. Created as simultaneously free and responsible, human freedom is nonetheless limited and fallible:

> In fact, man failed. He freely sinned. By refusing God's plan of love, he deceived himself and became a slave to sin. This first alienation engendered a multitude of others. From its outset, human history attests the wretchedness and oppression born of the human heart in consequence of the abuse of freedom.... The exercise of freedom does not imply a right to say or do everything. It is false to maintain that man, "the subject of this freedom," is "an individual who is fully self-sufficient and

---

13.   *Catechism*, nos. 1731-1732.

whose finality is the satisfaction of his own interests in the enjoyment of earthly goods.... By deviating from the moral law man violates his own freedom, becomes imprisoned within himself, disrupts neighborly fellowship, and rebels against divine truth.[14]

The vast range of understandings concerning human freedom is certainly not a recent development. Ancients sought to account for the abuse of freedom through myths, which sometimes attributed evil, and the resultant suffering and loss of true freedom, to conflicts among gods and goddesses, or sometimes portrayed the very existence of the material world and embodiment as a punishment for wicked behavior in the domain of the deities. In the case of "Pandora," the presence of evil in the world derives from an overwhelming feminine curiosity that resulted in Pandora's opening the box from which escaped a horde of calamities.

Through imagery-laden narratives, the Book of Genesis portrays human origins and the primal misuse of the divine gift of freedom by our progenitors. In conjunction with this, the historical developments of past millennia demonstrate the nexus among human freedom, limitation, and the ability of the human will to choose. The "question" of freedom always finds its particular expression within a given moment of history, within a given society or culture. Plato's eloquent description of human imprisonment within the "cave" of shadows had a context that not only spoke to his time, but bears meaning to all subsequent ages. The "cave" differs, but the imagery and truth proposed by Plato resonate strongly in the present age. In fact, the contemporary caves of the Middle East allow new elaborations of the theme.

---

14.   *Catechism*, nos. 1739-1740. See entire Article 3 on Human Freedom, nos. 1730-1748.

The *VR* user who dons a Head Mounted Display and technical glove (or wears the more streamlined glasses which allow more immediate passage into virtual environments) is seemingly "escaping" from imprisonment in the mundane, embodied, "real" world into worlds of freely chosen avatars and datascapes. The user may simply be sitting in a technical cave, *imprisoned by choice*, and vulnerable to influences that may soon exceed the conscious ability to control.

There is a climate of what may be termed "**boundary-lessness**" in the present time. There is a permissive climate, heady, often arrogant, and dismissive of any external measure or control—a cultural climate is not confined to *VR* laboratories and simulators. There is an *atmosphere*, an *ambience* or *aura* of unfettered virtual experience and technical application that has increasingly become a way of life for many. The desire to eliminate all boundaries as an expression of freedom brings resistance to whatever would restrain the *attempting of what is possible*. This seeming freedom is asserted 1) in a network of laboratory "caves" where research touching human, animal and plant life is conducted either with or without approval from responsible societal authorities; and 2) in the daily, digitalized world of communication, commercial enterprise, and entertainment. If there are carefully designed "caves of illusion," it can also be said that a "smog of virtuality" immerses the contemporary world. To live at the present time is to be immersed in aspects of the virtual, to breathe in aspects of the virtual simply by living in the opening years of the Third Millennium. Two examples will exemplify the elimination of boundaries in both biotechnical research and the commercial applications of scientific research.

In its "online" report for February 27, 2003, The BBC News Sci/Tech featured a Canadian company's experimental work on goats capable of producing spider's web protein in their milk. The company, using techniques similar to those

employed in the cloning of the sheep "Dolly," has bred goats
that have spider genes. The plan is to have the first two
goats, which have been genetically altered, sire countless
other goats that will produce milk containing the spider silk
protein. Since the naturally-occurring spider silk is the
toughest fibre known, with a tensile strength that is greater
than steel and yet twenty-five percent lighter than synthetic
petroleum-based polymers, the use of these animals could
"revolutionize" the materials industry, and other product-
lines such as bullet-proof clothing and aircraft.[15] There is no
indication in this report of concern for the integral being of
the "modified" goats, or of the company's having sought to
determine what such a crossing of species would mean.
There was also no indication that the company had submit-
ted its plans for such research to the wider national and
world community to determine whether or not such work
and its commercial applications should proceed. The only
long range effect suggested in the news report: plans to mass-
produce what has already been termed "biosteel." Further,
the report did not indicate a questioning of the crossing of
boundaries between species, or the boundaries between what
is "possible" and what should not proceed without responsible accountability to the world community in terms of trans-
species alterations that have massive ramifications.

Leon Kass writes:

> Organisms come into being through an orderly, self-
> directed process of differentiation that reaches an inter-
> nally determined end or completion. At each stage, but
> most fully when mature, each is an organic and active
> whole, a unity of structure and function, the parts con-
> tributing to the maintenance and working of the whole.

---

15.   See http://news.bbc.co.uk/1/hi/sci/tech/889951.stm, p.1.

> Wholeness is preserved through remarkable powers of self-healing, each organism acting unconsciously from within to restore its own integrity—which it somehow both "knows" and "wants".... Living things display directedness, inner "striving" toward a goal, activities that transcend confinement to the here and now.[16]

The surpassing of boundaries between the real and the virtual in commercial and entertainment venues is evident, as discussed above in regard to the projection of virtual environments. Flight simulators, video games, and increasingly sophisticated forms of *VE* may be described as intensified concentrations of virtuality. Benjamin Woolley's *Virtual Worlds* shows how pervasive the virtual has become and how the boundaries between real and unreal have been greatly dissolved. He appeals to descriptions given by Jean Baudrillard who wrote an article titled "The Gulf War will not take place," originally published in the French newspaper *Liberation* just before the Gulf War began.[17] Woolley points out how Baudrillard argued in the French press that the war was constituted through media coverage: "It was a postmodern

---

16. Leon Kass, *Life, Liberty and the Defense of Dignity: The Challenge for Bioethics* (San Francisco, 2002), pp 285-286. Kass then quotes from his former work, "Teleology, Darwinism, and the Place of Man: Beyond Chance and Necessity?" in *Toward a More Natural Science: Biology and Human Affairs* (New York, 1985): "A young bird will continue to struggle to coordinate wing and tail motions until it finally learns to fly. A beaver will make many trips to build a dam, or a bird a nest, or a spider a web.... And for many animals there is an elaborate pattern of behavior leading up to mating. *In none of these cases is the activity planned or conscious or intended, yet it is just the same a directed and inwardly determined activity to an end for a purpose.*" p. 256.
17. See Woolley, *Virtual Worlds*, pp.190ff for discussion of Baudrillard's insights.

war, a war where there is no reality, just, in Baudrillard's language, a simulation of it.... It was, he wrote, a 'virtual' war."[18] Baudrillard asserted that out of fear of the real, postmodernism has created a giant simulator in which reality no longer exists, in fact has *become* a fiction. In what Woolley terms a "classic essay on postmodernity," Baudrillard perceived a breakdown in reality that went through distinct historical stages concerning signification:

> ...the way signs are used—the way, say, a picture relates to what it depicts, or a sentence refers to whatever it is about—and they plot the gradual separation of the sign from what it signifies, the separation of culture from nature, 'truth' from reality. In the first stage, the sign reflects a basic reality, in the second, it hides that reality, and in the third it hides the *absence* of that reality...the final, and for Baudrillard terminal, stage, the stage of pure simulation, when signs cease to signify anything real. Culture is about producing signs that signify nothing, that have only spurious significance.[19]

The building of such a computerized, technically interconnected society came in the twentieth century when there was great disillusionment. Beginning with the smashing of the atom, the entire universe was opened in radically new ways. A tremendous, matter-centered explosion took place that was beyond containment. The intensity of swift energy-release, searing penetration, and incredible power was beyond familiar time-space containment. The contents of a twentieth-century Pandora's box, so infinitesimally small, had been unleashed, crossing boundaries previously not even recognized. The universe was radically changed for human-

---

18.   *Virtual Worlds*, p. 197.
19.   *Virtual Worlds*, p. 198.

ity. Other boundaries simultaneously began to give way. With the ability to grow in understanding DNA and genetic patterning, the boundaries of sexuality, marriage, and family were crossed with increasing frequency. It seemed that the meaning of all life—and the potential to change that meaning at will—were fields opened to limitless exploration and revamping to those who possessed the knowledge and equipment to trammel them. The fabrication of increasingly powerful instruments that penetrated the mysteries of subatomic particles was complemented by telescopes that gave promise of explaining the universe's origin, and space vehicles capable of placing humans on the moon. The "communications revolution" enabled such ventures, but also revolutionized economics, commerce, and entertainment, with all of the entities associated with them. Many adults who repeatedly jet across oceans, conduct business via cellular phones, store records in computer files, and attend sports events where huge televised images inform spectators of actions happening on the field, can still recall a childhood home that lacked electricity and running water, and was heated by a potbelly stove. The rapidity of change and the breaking of all familiar boundaries of experience over the past century resulted, for many, in 1) the seeming inevitability of relentless change; 2) the seeming irrelevance of former boundaries; and 3) the seeming destruction of enduring truths.

Some philosophical movements of the twentieth century that were concomitant with the swift breaking of boundaries intensified responses to these overwhelming changes. While many in Western society never formally studied philosophies that dismissed enduring truth and meaning, the ideas were "in the air" and pervaded daily experience. There was more frequent cynicism regarding what had been formerly believed, learned and observed. Concurrently there was a questioning: if so many familiar limitations had fallen away, had humanity been duped for millennia into thinking that there were limits, boundaries? With the 1960's came "open marriages," the flaunting of sexual deviations, and "The Theater of the Absurd."

At the extremity of philosophical theories, nihilism denied any basis for truth or knowledge. It rejected in general what were customary moral and religious beliefs. Nihilism denied meaning and purpose in existence. In an Internet posting of September 2002, a subscriber to this philosophy, simply signed as "Freydis," asserted that nihilism rejects belief in non-random events as well as the conviction that everything is structured toward a conclusive revelation. Nihilism rejects the idea of obedience toward a fulfilling destiny. Freydis says that there has never been evidence that the universe has a final purpose. Further:

> This is the simple beauty nihilism has that no other idea-set does. By breaking free from the tethers of ideology one is empowered in outlook and outcomes because for the first time it's possible to find answers without proceeding from pre-existing perceptions. We're finally free to find out what's really out there and not just the partial evidence to support original pretext [sic] and faulty notions making a hell on earth in the process.[20]

THE COINHERENCE OF FREEDOM AND TRUTH

The understanding of freedom is intrinsically related to truth. The ancient Greeks, in varying philosophical schools of thought, manifested a search for truth. It is impossible to know precisely what Pontius Pilate meant by his spontaneous question in reply to Jesus Christ's assertion that he came

---

20.   See freydis' website, <u>counterorder.com.</u>

to bear witness to the truth. "Truth? ... What is that?" (Jn. 18:38) Note that the attribution of this question to Pilate comes in the same Gospel where Jesus' identity is repeatedly expressed in relation to truth. Already in the Prologue of the Johannine Gospel, Jesus is confessed as the Word made flesh, who lived among us "full of grace and truth." (Jn. 1:14). To continue in Jesus' word means that His disciples will know the truth, and "the truth will make you free." (Jn. 8: 32) At the Last Supper, Jesus made a summary statement of identity: "I am the Way, the Truth, and the Life." (Jn. 14:6). He prayed to the Father for His disciples: "Consecrate them in the truth; your word is truth...for their sake I consecrate myself, so that they too may be consecrated in truth." (Jn. 17: 17, 19)

Until recent decades, there has been an acknowledged search for truth in Western civilization, as varied and controversial as the expressions of those searches have been. In a series of lectures delivered in Tubingen and the University of Munich between 1947-1949, Romano Guardini masterfully synthesized the predominant periods of development in Western civilization. Published under the title *The End of the Modern World*, and re-published at the turn into the Third Millennium, Guardini's lectures reveal his prescient insight. After cryptically describing the periods of classical antiquity, the Middle Ages, and the Modern Period, he showed why there was a disjuncture that eventuated in "the end of the modern world." In doing so, Guardini has been proven prophetic in foreseeing developments within Western nations. In particular, he showed how the understandings of *nature, personality,* and *culture* in the Modern Age resulted in a rejection of both God and a divine revelation that has enduring meaning. A new and purely secular set of values came with the Modern Age.

In decades preceding the Second World War, motivated by technology, the "technical man" sought to take possession of nature, not experiencing it as having a standard of value or seeing it as a "shelter for his spirit." Guardini said:

> The technological mind sees nature as an insensate order, as a cold body of facts, as a mere "given," as an object of utility, as raw material to be hammered into useful shape; it views the cosmos similarly as a mere "space" into which objects can be thrown with complete indifference. Technological man will remold the world; he sees his task as Promethean and its stakes as being and non-being.[21]

Guardini asserted that with the dissolution of the Modern Age, there was a rejection of Revelation. With that rejection, "genuine personality" also disappeared from human consciousness. He stated that the coming era would bring a precision of what this meant in ways that would be frightful and salutary. "Since Revelation is not a subjective experience but a simple Truth promulgated by Him who also made the world, every moment of history which excludes that Revelation is threatened in its most hidden recesses."[22] Guardini's synthesis predated major technological developments of the past five and a half decades. His perceptiveness, however, in seeing how matter, living beings and the human person would be used, reads at times like a handbook of what would occur in the six decades following his analyses. The paganism of the future, he said, would be different from pre-Christian paganism, which did not have the opportunity of knowing Christ. Dogma "in its very nature, however, surmounts the march of time because it is rooted in eternity.... Christianity will once again need to prove itself deliberately

---

21.   Romano Guardini, *The End of the Modern World* (Wilmington, 1998), p. 55.

22.   *The End of the Modern World*, p. 100.

as a faith which is not self-evident; it will be forced to distinguish itself more sharply from a dominantly non-Christian ethos."[23]

Interestingly, Guardini said that *danger* would be the characteristic mark of the soon-to-emerge culture, a danger that would arise from the culture itself, arising from man. "Science and technology have so mastered the forces of nature that destruction, either chronic or acute and incalculable in extent, is now a possibility. Without exaggeration, one can say that a new era of history has been born. Now and forever man will live at the brink of an ever-growing danger which shall leave its mark upon his entire existence."[24]

It needs to be re-emphasized that Guardini was speaking of cultural dissolution occurring at the conclusion of the Second World War. In describing how the understandings of *nature, personality* and *culture* changed, he said that in the intellectual consciousness of modern Europe there were three ideals: "a Nature subsisting in itself; an autonomous personality of the human subject; a culture self-created out of norms intrinsic to its own essence."[25] Such "ideals" seemingly held promise of unlimited possibility, without reference or responsibility to a Being or source beyond self-determination. What Guardini foretold has strikingly come to be an accurate description of world conditions in the opening years of the Third Millennium. Danger has become a predominant characteristic of the age, and its multiple manifestations emerge from using nature as an "insensate order, as a cold body of facts, as a mere 'given,' as an object of utility, as raw material to be hammered into useful shape."

---

23.   *The End of the Modern World*, p. 106.
24.   *The End of the Modern World*, pp. 90-91.
25.   *The End of the Modern World*, p. 50.

Weapons of mass destruction, whether nuclear, biological or chemical, have become incalculable in their potential for immense and enduring deadliness. What is less evident: the dangers emanating from research laboratories and clinics in which genetic manipulation and multiple forms of self-determined experimentation occur.

LOOKING TO THE BEGINNING

If the fundamental truths of Revelation concerning the meaning and destiny of nature, persons, and culture are considered non-existent or irrelevant in the development of the future, how does contemporary theology meet its responsibility? From the earliest years of his pontificate, Pope John Paul II addressed the task at hand. Similar to the manner in which Jesus Christ dealt with foundational questions concerning marriage and human meaning, John Paul said that it was essential to "look to the beginning" in order to understand the divine intent in the creation of humanity. Progressively, in audiences, encyclicals, personal journeys and writings, he continued to address fundamental issues in relation to the Divine *economia*, the Divine Plan that encompasses the meaning of the entire universe entrusted to the stewardship of man and woman and which gives immense dignity to all of creation. Punctuating the works of John Paul are certain landmark documents, however, that touch directly upon the mounting issues raised by virtual reality.

On the Feast of the Transfiguration in 1993, John Paul issued his encyclical *Veritatis Splendor*, "The Splendor of Truth." The preliminary words to the document read: "The splendour of truth shines forth in all the works of the Creator and, in a special way, in man, created in the image and likeness of God (cf. *Gen.* 1:26). Truth enlightens man's intelligence and shapes his freedom, leading him to know and love the Lord."[26] Clearly, at the outset, John Paul specifies the unity between freedom and truth. His purpose in writing the encyclical, the Pope noted, was that "a new situation has come about *within the Christian community itself,* which has experienced the spread of numerous doubts and objections of a human and psychological, social and cultural, religious and even properly theological nature, with regard to the Church's moral teachings."[27] At the root of dissent from traditional moral teaching, he wrote, were presuppositions influenced by currents of thought "which end by detaching human freedom from its essential and constitutive relationship to truth." (Art. 4)

Pope John Paul II saw that it was necessary to clarify foundational principles for moral teaching based in Scripture and tradition, but also to shed light on the presuppositions and consequences of those who opposed the Church's moral teaching. Influenced by subjectivism and individualism, certain tendencies in contemporary moral theology lessen or deny *the dependence of freedom on truth.* (Cf. Art. 34) While a heightened appreciation for the dignity of the human person has occurred, John Paul said, some now hold the conviction that human freedom has been exalted to an absolute, and that *it* is the source of all values. (Cf. Art. 31, 32) Alleging that there is a conflict between divine law and human freedom, certain individuals and groups claim the right to determine good and evil.

---

26.   Pope John Paul II, *Veritatis Splendor,* complete text in *Considering Veritatis Splendor,* John Wilkins ed. (Cleveland, Ohio, 1994), p. 82.

27.   *Veritatis Splendor,* Art. 4. Hereafter, citations from the encyclical will be noted by Article, within the text.

Human freedom would thus be able to "create values" and would enjoy a primacy over truth, to the point that truth itself would be considered a creation of freedom. Freedom would thus lay claim to a *moral autonomy* which would actually amount to an *absolute sovereignty.* (Art. 35)

Far from divine law denying human freedom, John Paul wrote, it promotes and defends its authenticity. This involves an anomaly. Along with the elevated respect for freedom in the contemporary world, there is a radical questioning of the very existence of human freedom. John Paul not only refers to the "conditioning" delineated in the behavioral sciences, but also to "theories which misuse scientific research about the human person." (Art. 33) The setting of opposition between *freedom and truth* manifests a still further dichotomy: a claimed opposition between *faith and morality.*

Faith has content, not constituted by a set of propositions but by what John Paul terms "an act of trusting abandonment to Christ" (Art. 88) that enables a human person to live as Christ did in love of God and neighbor, even to the point of martyrdom. Those schools of moral theory that retain a stance of relativity in the discernment of good and evil, and which deny that the objects of certain moral acts are intrinsically evil, are in error. Human acts are morally good only when they are *in conformity with man's true good* and thus express the voluntary ordering of the person toward his ultimate end: God himself, the supreme good in whom man finds his full and perfect happiness. (Cf. Art. 72)

In a sense, many things which were formerly "unthinkable" in ordinary human experience have become familiar, routine: "Smart Bombs," surgery performed at a distance via televised imagery; and audible messages transmitted from men walking on the surface of the moon. Within the time frame of a few decades, such phenomenal occurrences (and they are) can easily foster a conviction that technology can enable the crossing of any boundary—physical, hormonal, or mental. "Relativity" has become a term that not only applies to Einstein's theory but also describes the qualities of indefiniteness, reversibility, boundarylessness, and unpredictability that pervade contemporary human experience. In fact, these qualities are sought with varying degrees of avidity, particularly in the affluent societies of the contemporary world. One evident result of affinity for that which is relative and easily changeable is the hesitation that many experience today concerning the possibility of making permanent commitments, whether this be in covenantal marriage, in a demanding profession, or the long-term care of someone in need.

There is particular attraction, then, in what is "virtual"—in what can be fashioned, re-fashioned, experienced simultaneously in a variety of ways, or exterminated at will. "Animated cartoons" (a telling phrase) give the impression that simulated figures can be altered, catapulted, exploded in one sequence, and then reappear in an endless series of escapes, beatings and deaths. The observation of Benjamin Woolley bears repeating here: "We are like cartoon characters who have walked off a cliff edge and, still suspended in the air, have suddenly realized that there is nothing beneath us. This is the crisis of postmodernity, and it is technology which has produced it."

In the Introduction to *The Pearly Gates of Cyberspace*, Margaret Wertheim notes that similar to the late Roman era, the contemporary scene is marked by inequity, corruption and fragmentation.[28] While fragmentation and interchangeability are ordinary, they can also evoke an interest in religion. Cyberspace is not an outcome of any theological

---

28.   See Margaret Wertheim, *The Pearly Gates of Cyberspace: A History of Space from Dante to the Internet*, (New York, 1999), p. 22.

system, but for many, it takes on a kind of spiritual appeal, apart from what are perceived as the constraints of organized religions. For certain groups, says Margaret Wertheim, interaction with elements in cyberspace has special attraction. Boys, for example, who are experiencing a time of particular bodily awkwardness find it desirable. Likewise, certain women and members of racial minorities whose bodies seem to evoke bias can find that virtual interaction provides a way of escaping the relentless "bodily scrutiny" that marks contemporary American life. Baldness, acne, and obesity are seemingly left behind "in the 'messy' world," and "Some champions of cyberspace dream of escaping entirely from 'the ballast of materiality,' or what one commentator has called the 'cloddishness' of the body."[29] There can seem to be security in donning the paraphernalia of *VE* and fashioning, refashioning, and interacting with virtual avatars. As indicated earlier, however, the experience can also be radically disorienting.

CRITICAL ISSUES FOR THEOLOGICAL REFLECTION

Why should matters such as virtual avatars, cyborgs, and journeys into cyberspace be of urgent concern for theologians? As shown throughout the present work, the virtual environment is not restricted to sophisticated military simulators or research centers. Since the entire "climate of life" in contemporary Western nations is increasingly permeated with elements of the virtual, it necessarily must be of importance for theology. John Macquarrie has explained that there are six formative factors that are almost universally operative in theology: experience, revelation, Scripture, tradition, rea-

---

29.   *The Pearly Gates of Cyberspace*, p. 25.

son and culture. This is not equivalent, says Macquarrie, to following a recipe in which one would take a little revelation, add a little reason, etc. and "shake well together." Rather, it is a matter of taking into account the tensions among these factors that contribute to theology in order to avoid one-sided simplifications. Regarding the factor of culture, Macquarrie notes the need for a fine balance between 1) accommodating revelation to the mood of the time, and 2) "so insulating the revelation against all contact with the changing forms of secular culture" to the point where "it becomes encapsulated."[30]

When there is urgency expressed in this book concerning the significant theological issues raised by virtual reality, (issues which pertain particularly to experience, culture and reason) that urgency is always proffered in relation to the more fundamental factors that are formative of theology: revelation, Scripture, tradition. The desire is *wholeness*. Jesus Christ urged awareness of the "signs of the times." Macquarrie pointed out the need to "frankly acknowledge the cultural factor in theology, and try to handle it in full awareness of its potentialities. If we try to exclude this factor, then it will work unconsciously, for it is inescapable."[31]

A further clarification is in order here. When "the new" emerges within a given culture, or in human society generally, its very unfamiliarity may prove discomfiting. That can lead to a total rejection of "the new" or at least a skeptical, critical approach to it. While the emphasis in this work is critical recognition of the urgent theological questions arising from virtual reality and its developing possibilities, there

---

30.   John Macquarrie, *Principles of Christian Theology,* 2nd ed. (New York, 1977) p. 15. See pp. 1-18 for a synthesis of his thought on the formative factors of theology.

31.   *Principles of Christian Theology,* p. 15.

are aspects that need to be considered from a positive perspective as well. It must be asked: *Why* has this potential emerged with such insistence at this time? Why does it hold such fascination? What benefits have accrued from the responsible utilization of "the virtual"? More deeply, however, it must be asked what an increasing environment of virtuality means for human life and responsible stewardship and creativity. In order to question more deeply, however, *why* these fascinating possibilities also present significant theological issues, it is important to consider three specific aspects of the "virtual" which have direct bearing on theological understanding of Catholic faith: *avatars, cyborgs,* and *cyberspace.*

AVATARS AND INCARNATIONAL REALITY

From ancient times, religious and philosophical systems have incorporated the possibility of "Avatars." The ancient Greek *pleroma,* for example, was considered to be a vast inter-space between a distant divinity and cosmic material beings. Although ancient Gnostic systems of thought differed, adherents believed that the *pleroma* was inhabited by *aeons* and *demiurges* of varying ranks—neither totally divine nor human. Myths associated with these intermediaries between the divine and the human were part of a larger attempt to understand and explain "how things were." According to some Gnostic groups, the intermediaries sometimes assumed the appearance of "avatars" in order to associate with human beings. There was no totally cohesive system among those who thought of the *pleroma* as a place where superhuman beings effected some interchange between a remote god and the world of daily life on earth.[32] Avatars also figured in the belief systems of some Eastern religions, and followers of occult practices speak of shape-shifting. So, the assuming of temporary "bodies" or "forms" is not a novelty introduced by technology.

The real-body, the lived body, is a fundamental aspect of Catholic faith. The New Testament is constant witness to Jesus Christ's true incarnation, genuine earthly life, and enduring presence in resurrection. Already within the first Christian century there were attempts to contest this. Cipriano Vagaggini shows how the Pauline Letters, the Letter to the Hebrews, and the Johannine corpus in the New Testament have a polemical quality in their defense of the actuality of Jesus Christ's birth, public life, suffering, death and resurrection. Vagaggini states as a general principle that "the co-essential and *permanent* function of Jesus' body in the transmission to us of the divine life is then the accomplishment of our salvation." For this transmission to be effected, there had to be a way of making it possible for every concrete person to come into contact with salvation. It was the Eucharist above all that ensured this. Vagaggini comments on the sixth chapter of John's Gospel:

> To eat the flesh of Christ is the same as "eating Christ": the expression "who eats my flesh" of verse 56 is the equivalent of "who eats me" in verse 57.

> Eating the flesh of Christ brings about the union between Christ and the person who eats: Christ dwells in him and he in Christ. Here, in terms of a reciprocal abode, John expresses what St. Paul meant in terms of *koinonia*. This reciprocal penetration includes the transmission of the divine life that fills Christ from the Father and

---

32.   See Steve Kellmeyer, "The New Gnostic Gospel" in *Envoy Magazine*, vol. 4.5, pp. 34-39, for a compact analysis of the film *The Matrix* in relation to ancient Gnosticism.

is communicated by Christ to men through the eating of his flesh.

> Christ's flesh appears as the living vehicle of the transmission of the divine life from the Father through Christ to the one who eats Christ. This explains why Christ's very flesh, the Word of God made flesh, is completely penetrated with the divine life as is his whole human nature. St. Paul had said that in him dwelt the fullness of divinity *somatikos*. Therefore the flesh is alive with divine life and gives this same life to one who eats it.[33]

There can be no question here of a projected body, of an avatar, or a "seeming body." It must be emphasized again that, according to John 6, Christ's promise of total self-gift in His real body and blood became the watershed moment of decision for those who heard His promise. Most of those who heard Him say that *He* was the real food and drink that had been foreshadowed by the manna made the decision to leave His company. At the Last Supper He inaugurated the realization of that assertion, handing over His body and blood as gift in perpetuity.

The reality of Jesus Christ's body and blood, now in resurrected and perpetual self-gift, remains the critical point. Any reductionist interpretation of His living and personal reality loses not only the truth of Jesus Christ but the full truth of what it means to be human. This above all other considerations explains why virtual reality focuses the most fundamental issues for theology in the beginning years of the Third Millennium.

It has been pointed out how thoroughly "the virtual" pervades daily life on earth. Fiction has been a major avenue

---

33.   Cipriano Vagaggini, *The Flesh: Instrument of Salvation* (Staten Island, New York, 1969) pp. 60-61.

for alerting readers to these levels of the virtual. How much "before their times," for example, are the works of Lewis Carroll that portray a curious "Alice" crossing through the "looking-glass" and entering "spaces" where ordinary sizes and shapes do not apply, where creatures and communications change unpredictably and lack meaningful context. Similarly, there is a prophetic quality to the film *The Purple Rose of Cairo,* which featured a woman obsessed with a film star. Each day after work she would go to the movie theater to see films in which her "hero" (and her fantasy lover) starred. One evening, as she intently watches the film, the actor seemingly steps out of the picture, comes to her and begins a relationship. Each of these narrative forms, the Carroll novel and the film, involves a two-way crossing of the boundary between reality and a subjective world created in the imagination. Fictively, there is a dissolving of boundaries from both "sides." Novels, live theater, and "special-effects films" can delight, can bring a freshness to daily life. Participation in increasingly sophisticated forms of "the virtual," however, can bring about a disorientation and loss of *the capacity to know the difference between the real and the unreal, at least for a time.* This differs from participation in creative works that evoke insight and bring freshness and re-creative élan to the realities of daily life.

MULTIPLE IMPLICATIONS FOR FAITH AND THEOLOGICAL REFLECTION

So it is crucial to realize that the issue of assuming *avatars* concerns not only the contemporary embodied human person, but also the reality of Jesus Christ: His incarnation, His earthly life, and His Paschal self-gift now effective in the sacramental life of the Church. As pointed out earlier, *Gaudium et spes*, Article #22 affirms an intimate bond between the reality of Jesus' incarnate, enduring presence and the meaning of every human person's bodily presence:

> He who is the "image of the invisible God" (Col. 1:15) is himself the perfect man who has restored in the children of Adam that likeness to God which had been disfigured ever since the first sin. Human nature, by the very fact that it was assumed, not absorbed, in him, has been raised in us also to a dignity beyond compare. For, by his incarnation, he, the son of God, has in a certain way united himself with each man. He worked with human hands, he thought with a human mind. He acted with a human will, and with a human heart he loved. Born of the Virgin Mary, he has truly been made one of us, like to us in all things except sin.

There is an enduring reality of the *one physical body* of Jesus Christ, through all phases of its development and glorification. From the beginning of Christian witness, there has been an emphasis on His bodily reality, distinguishing Christian faith regarding Jesus Christ from Gnostic and docetic teachings that would have accommodated understanding of the Incarnation to a "seeming" bodily manifestation. Already in the Pauline *Corpus* and the Johannine writings there is an emphasis on Jesus' enduring physical reality.[34] When that is misunderstood, the way is opened to aberrations concerning every revealed truth expressed in the Deposit of Faith. There is need for renewed emphasis and clarification regarding the enduring reality of Christ's true bodiliness lest it be confused with "avatars." This applies not only to His conception and

---

34. See Vagaggini's *The Flesh: Instrument of Salvation*, pp. 31-45, where the author stresses this. Early in the Church's experience, he says, one already finds a "polemical" stance toward any teaching that would diminish the full reality of Christ's physical body.

birth, but also to significant experiences revealed in Scripture, such as His transfiguration, His post-resurrection appearances, and His real presence in the Eucharist. The *immersion* in a contemporary milieu that favors "fluid boundaries" between what is real and what is unreal can result in uncertainties regarding truths of the faith—most centrally, those regarding authentic understanding of the Eucharist.

In the previous chapter there was reference to a diminishment of belief in the Real Presence of Christ in the Blessed Sacrament. The results of a Gallup poll conducted among Catholics in the United States a few years ago to determine their Eucharistic belief astounded many. The poll showed that there is serious confusion among Catholics concerning the reality of the Real Presence. Only 30 percent of those polled indicated that they believed they truly received the Body and Blood, soul and divinity of Jesus Christ under the appearance of bread and wine when they received Holy Communion. Another 29 percent said that they think of the "bread and wine" only as Jesus' spirit and teaching: to receive the elements expresses their attachment to His person and words. Ten percent indicated that their belief involved receiving bread and wine in which Jesus is present. Still another 23 percent think that the bread and wine become Christ's Body and Blood *because of their personal belief.*[35] The confusion among Catholics concerning the Eucharist, evident among many who responded to this poll, is indicative of the need for clarity concerning Jesus Christ's personal identity, the reality of His enduring personal presence, and the meaning of eating His Body and Blood.

---

35.   See Archbishop Michael J. Sheehan, "Is the Eucharist Really Christ's Body and Blood?" http://www.petersnet/browse/1340.htm, p.1.

The four Dogmatic Constitutions of the Second Vatican Council stressed in various ways how the understanding of the mysteries of faith revealed in Jesus Christ is intimately linked with understanding of the human person. The problem, perhaps, does not so much reside *basically* in Eucharistic belief as it does in grasping the meaning, dignity and mystery of the embodied person. Analogously, when it seems possible, after stepping "through the looking-glass" of a virtual reality interface to project multiple avatars in cyberspace and to identify/interact with them, the matter of Real Presence in the Eucharist can diminish in importance.

In Jesus' Last Discourse (Jn. 14-17), there is the fullest revelation concerning the inner life of God. In a most intimate manner, Jesus revealed to those at table with Him not only his profound relationship with the Father, but also basic aspects of inner Trinitarian life. He revealed that the inner life of God is a *Communion of Persons.* The reality of that Communion of Life, He revealed, is Self-Gift, received and fully reciprocated among the Three Persons. The manifestation of that divine life within humanity reaches its fullest expression in His own self-gift in the Body and Blood, given perpetually.

CYBORGS

The conjoining of human bodies and technological hard and software is not new. In 1989, Father Robert Brungs described the growing surety that it could be accomplished. He wrote:

> A cyborg is the ultimate Six Million Dollar Man, the symbiotic mating of a human brain with a machine body. As such, it represents the ultimate stage in the technologization of the human being. Again, there is no near pros-

pect of this human-machine union being achieved, but attitudes about the meaning of human being and human living are far and away the most important ingredient in biotechnological development.[36]

The complete fusion of human-technological devices has not been achieved instantaneously. It is, rather, advancing by degrees. Already in 1989 Brungs listed ways in which bio-technologies were being used "to influence, enhance and finally control those capacities which we consider to be the most human: speech, thought, choice, emotion, memory, imagination, creativity and, perhaps, spiritual vision."[37] At the time of Brungs's observations, there already were people who had minute implants in their bodies, allowing portions of their bodies to be under radio control.

At the University of Reading in 1998, Professor Kevin Warwick and his team in the Department of Cybernetics set out to answer the question "What happens when a man is merged with a computer?" In "Project Cyborg," Warwick had a "silicon chip transponder" surgically implanted into his arm, allowing a computer to monitor him as he walked through halls and moved through the Cybernetics Department. He was able to operate doors, lights, heaters and other computers "without lifting a finger."[38] In March 2002, "Project Cyborg 2.0" began. This phase is exploring how a new implant "could send signals back and forth between Warwick's nervous system and a computer."[39] If this succeeds, the plan is to implant a similar chip in Warwick's wife,

---

36. Robert Brungs, *You See Lights Breaking Upon Us: Doctrinal Perspectives on Biological Advance* (St. Louis, Missouri, 1989), p. 21.
37. Ibid.
38. "Project Cyborg 1.0," http://www.rdg.ac.uk/KevinWarwick/html/project_cyborg_1_0.html.
39. Ibid.

Irena, in order to see how movement, thought or emotion signals could also be transmitted from person to person.

Steve Mizrach points out that the merger of human and technological device is not simply a dramatic leap realized in a research facility. Beyond bionic prostheses and bio-implants, the Human Genome Initiative allowed those who operated DNA sequencers to practice positive eugenics in ways previously unrealizable. The literature explaining the new "bioelectronics" and "cyborg bioethics" makes clear that the intermesh of human and artifact has been happening gradually, imperceptibly. Pacemakers, hormone-producing implants and heart transplants have made merger of person and machine familiar, although most people probably do not think of them as moving toward an increasingly realized cyborg.

The military, in particular, is cited in this literature for its work on producing the soldier who can think, react, and communicate with augmented capacities. In fact, "augmentation" is a word used frequently in relation to the construction of a cyborg. Mizrach says that for science fiction writers in the 1960's, a *cyborg* meant a sort of hybrid, "a mesh of flesh and steel, neurons and wires, blood and circuits." From *The Six Million Dollar Man* to *Robocop*, says Mizrach, "the question posed by all these depictions of the cyborg was, how much of a human being could you replace and still preserve its essential humanity?"[40] Mirach writes that in the 1990's debates over biotechnology, four constructs were reaching unprecedented unification: eugenics, technologizing the body, the cyborg, and the augmentation machine. After the dissociation of eugenics from Nazism and the dis-

---

40.　Steve Mizrach, "Should there be a limit placed on the integration of humans and computers and electronic technology?" http://www.limmat.ch/koni/texte/cyborg-ethics.html, p. 3.

covery of DNA, it was possible to manipulate and isolate techniques of biological change, separating them from sexual reproduction. He says further:

> The integration of biological and electronic processes suggests that they may be very similar in their mode of operation, and only based on different physical constituents. For most people, this touches on fundamental issues of what it means to be human. Most people assume that they have attributes machines do not (free will, emotions, a soul) but will these beliefs hold up as electronic technology becomes "hardwired" into human organisms? ... People today are openly speaking about post-biological man. The technological and the organic are colliding in mysterious ways. Silicon neural networks are being modeled on the human brain and artificial life algorithms are simulating in microseconds the millennium-long processes of evolution and natural selection.... The human cyborg represents a "transitional species" of sorts, before the human enters total post-biological obsolescence....[41]

In "You Are Cyborg," Hari Kunzru cites Norbert Wiener, who wrote *Cybernetics, or Control and Communication in the Animal and Machine* in 1948. A MIT mathematician, Wiener took the term "cybernetics" from the Greek *kubernetes,* meaning "steersman." Followers of Wiener took up the term for the science that would explain feedback systems, allowing control of "just about anything" from bodies to factories:

> The cyborgmakers were in the business of making Wiener's ideas flesh. For them, the body was just a meat computer running a collection of information systems

---

41.   Mizrach, "Should there be a limit..." pp. 2,3, and 4.

that adjusted themselves in response to each other and their environment. If you wanted to make a better body, all you had to do was improve the feedback mechanisms, or plug in another system—an artificial heart, an all-seeing bionic eye. It's no accident that this strangely abstract picture of the body as a collection of networks sounds rather like that other network of networks, the Internet; both came out of the same hothouse of Cold War military research.[42]

Two aspects of cyborg development are evident: 1) cyborg development began more than fifty years ago and is not simply science fiction; and 2) the transformative impact of cyborgization on the body-person is happening *incrementally* so that the magnitude of human change is not generally perceived as problematic.[43]

If, as Benedict Ashley says, *every* question that one can ask has some reference to the body,[44] the growing capacity to merge the body-person with machines and/or animal life should be raising multiple questions that preclude postponement. In light of the Incarnation, the Paschal Mystery, and the enduring meaning of Christ's physical body and every human body, there is an inescapable responsibility not only to be cognizant of processes that treat the lived body as "just a meat computer running a collection of information systems," but also to respond to them cogently. In the so-called

---

42. Henri Kunzru, "You Are Cyborg" in *Wired Digital, Inc.* 5:02 (February, 1997), p. 8.

43. Cf. Mary T. Prokes, "The Body: Precious Sacramental or Processed Artifact?" in *The National Catholic Bioethics Quarterly*, Vol. 3, No. 1 (Spring 2003), pp. 139-162.

44. See Benedict Ashley, *Theologies of the Body: Humanist and Christian* (Braintree, Massachusetts, 1985), p. 4.

"augmentation" of the human body-person, *what boundaries may not be crossed* concern:

- Identification as human being, as belonging to the human race
- Personal genomic identity
- Uniqueness of person
- Authenticity of free will and the capacity for personal responsibility
- Capacity for authentic human relationship
- Reality of immortal soul, divinely given and destined for eternal life

Each of these crucial matters (related as they are) requires careful attention. They are not speculative topics that refer to a remote future: they apply immediately to ongoing research and to multiple applications for every living human being—indeed, for all creation.

CYBERSPACE

Stephen Jones asks "...what exactly is cyberspace/VRspace? Is it a dream world? Is it some sort of trance space? And is the artist/producer of cyberspaces akin to the shaman in tribal culture?" It does have those characteristics for many, he says, "largely because one is removed from the world when taking on the helmet and harness of the VR installation."[45]

The interrelated meaning of *space* and *place* is basic to a worldview, which is a fundamental stance within the cosmos.

---

45.   Stephen Jones, "Towards a Philosophy of Virtual Reality," p. 2, http://www.immersence.com/publications/Sjones_B.html.

How radically have worldviews changed over the past two millennia! The poet(s) of Psalm 19 and Psalm 8 wrote of "the vault of heaven" (Ps. 19:1) and observed, "I look up at your heavens, made by your fingers, at the moon and stars you set in place."(Ps. 8:3) For the ancients, it seemed that the earth was fixed on a foundation that would not be moved and that a solid dome enclosed the visible rounding of space. In contrast, there is in the present decade a kind of "rolling revision" of theories concerning the size, composition, and rate of expansion of the universe, as newly obtained data are reviewed. "By studying the light of some 800 rare pulsating stars, a team recently calculated that for every 3.26 million light-years distant an object is from Earth, it is moving away 160,000 miles an hour faster. Such knowledge helps to establish the age and fate of the universe."[46] The "contemporary worldview" includes relativity, explosive change, and the measurement of astronomical distances and speeds.

Yet, daily life seems so firm and calculable: skyscrapers thrust upward solidly from an earth that is swirling on its axis, and the swallows still return to Capistrano each March 19. The astounding combinations within real space and place are dumbfounding and can only be comprehended at minuscule levels. Together with the incredible realities of the cosmos that are constantly being opened to human consciousness and exploration, there are the technological tools of "the virtual." An anomaly emerges here: While the unfathomable events of the *real universe* become better known and more expansive, the *virtual universe* tends to shrink to a constricted "space" prepared for fantasy environments and virtual interactions. Suzanne Ackers suggests:

---

46.   Kathy Sawyer, "Unveiling the Universe," in *National Geographic*, Millennium Supplement: The Universe, Vol. 196, 4 (October, 1999), p. 27.

...Renaissance perspective is displaced, and we are learning new ways of seeing, navigating in new kinds of conceptual space. Point of view no longer operates in its traditional manner. It now alters over time, and our perception of time and space becomes a virtual knowledge, no longer fixed to the Cartesian frame: mutable, always recalculated, determined by our progress through the environment. Consciousness can only follow along, hoping to make the necessary adjustments before we fallout [sic] of the world. Our internal center is temporarily dislocated from our external center, suddenly we do not know where we are.[47]

Real space and place are not indifferent aspects of human existence. They have enduring significance, as does the integrity of the real person, expressed bodily in space and time. Philip Sheldrake describes "place" as particular space that is able to be remembered and "to evoke what is most precious." It engages a person's identity, relationships and history.[48] Sheldrake refers to Walter Brueggermann's insightful commentary:

Place is space which has historical meanings, where some things have happened which are now remembered and which provide continuity and identity across generations. Place is space in which important words have been spoken which have established identity, defined vocation and envisioned destiny. Place is space in which vows have been exchanged, promises have been made, and demands have been issued. Place is indeed a protest against an unpromising pursuit of space. It is a declaration that our

---

47. See S. Jones, "Toward a Philosophy of Virtual Reality," p. 5.
48. See Philip Sheldrake, "Human Identity and the Particularity of Place," *Spiritus: A Journal of Christian Spirituality* 1:1 (2001), pp. 1-4, in http://muse.jhu.edu/demos/scs/1.1sheldrake.html.

humanness cannot be found in escape, detachment, absence of commitment, and undefined freedom...whereas pursuit of space may be a flight from history, a yearning for a place is a decision to enter history with an identifiable people in an identifiable pilgrimage.[49]

Such qualities of space and place are (at least temporarily) obliterated in the subjective, ever-open-to-revision fabrications of virtual environments in cyberspace. Once they are terminated by the person(s) who are fashioning them, virtual "spaces" and "places" evaporate; they no longer exist as realities that relate to living persons, their roots or their relationships. Even in the programming of virtual experiences for purposes of education, there is a certain disjuncture between the actual and the virtual. For example, a flight simulator condenses space and place. An airline pilot can practice difficult maneuvers within its confines, and integrate physical movement and decision-making in ways that will indeed affect his/her body-person in later circumstances, allowing helpful preparation for later actual flights. How different this is, however, from the factual distances, weather conditions (or, in the case of military pilots, even hostile gunfire) in real space and time that will affect actual flight. After a training session in a flight simulator, a pilot can step from the electronically wired module into a well-lit hallway, drive away in the family automobile, and arrive home in a short time. In a sense, what transpired in the simulator evaporates. In less dramatic ways, the same pilot experiences multiple "artificial" reductions of time and place in everyday life.

---

49.   Walter Brueggemann, *The Land: Place as Gift, Promise and Challenge in Biblical Faith* (Philadelphia: Fortress, 1977.), p. 5, cited in Sheldrake, "Human Identity," p. 3.

Sheldrake cites a term coined by French anthropologist Marc Auge: *non-place.* Auge uses it to designate locations that do *not* mark memory, give identity, or foster relationship. Examples of such "non-places" include airports, department stores, hotels, and highways. There is a disconcerting quality of the virtual about them. It is possible to be in a neighborhood shopping mall or to walk through an airport concourse and, momentarily at least, have the vague feeling "of being in no particular place on earth." The airport concourse and shops could be replicated in Denver, Rome, or Minneapolis. In that same vein, after one emerges from a darkened theater after seeing a gripping film, there is a momentary dazed realization that one is surrounded once more by the prosaic, the familiar and real: customers purchasing popcorn, a cold wind whisking through the entrance doors, and passersby hurrying past, intent on their errands. So, the common experiences of attending a film or shopping at a mega-mall already involve multiple aspects of the "virtual." These can dull sensibility to the unique and make the realities of space and place also seem indifferent.

It is said that following a visit to a suburban area of California, the poetess Gertrude Stein commented, "There was no there *there*." Her wry observation accords with Sheldrake's saying that mobility and centralization have brought about a relativity of space that diminishes a human sense of it. In fact, he says, *to remain* in a given place is perceived as the lot of those who are deprived in some way—the poor, the aged, and those with disabilities.

Why should such characteristics of cyberspace be of concern to persons of faith and theologians seeking an understanding of faith in the Third Millennium? Are these cyberspace characteristics not also the attributes of dreams, fantasies, and creative imagination? To a certain extent, that is so. Two things need to be noted, however. First, in the deliberate projection of virtual interactive environments, there is a disjuncture between the *real* and the electronically induced *virtual* that far exceeds "the suspension of disbelief" that occurs when participating in capably produced theater productions, novels, and other aesthetic forms. Second, and more importantly, for some working in the development of the virtual, there is the desire to transform the human body in conjunction with "intelligent machines" in a secular milieu that devalues the preciousness of space and place.

Central to Christian faith is the reality of the Incarnation—the Divine Word, the Second Person of the Blessed Trinity becoming flesh and blood in a definite place at a given moment of history. The prologue of John's Gospel proclaims the Word as being "with God" from all eternity, of "being sent" into the world, to His "domain." That is to say that the revelations of Jesus Christ occur at specific places and that, to this day, they bear enduring significance. The small village of Cana in Galilee, for example, is enduringly marked by the first Sign of Jesus, His changing water into wine at a wedding feast. Similarly, the exchanges between Jesus and the woman at the well in Samaria include a clarification regarding "places" of authentic worship: the mountain of Gerizim; Jerusalem; and ultimately the living embodied divine Person—the "I am"—who asks for a drink of water. Note how the Gospels refer to specific names, distances, and times. The Sea of Galilee is forever marked by the presence and miracles of Jesus, as are Bethany, Capharnaum, and the Kedron Valley. Each of these is marked as a place of sacred, enduring significance.

Chapters fourteen through seventeen of John's Gospel fuse Jesus' prayer to the Father with intimate revelatory dialogue with His Apostles. The Last Discourse deals with mutual indwelling, the possibility of living within one another. Note how this deepens and changes the significance of place and space. The specifics of Incarnational realities make it impossible to be indifferent or dismissive of "place."

Rather, they introduce into cosmic history an entirely new meaning of *sacred place* and *sacred spaces*, and they take their significance mainly from the manner in which the bodily Presence of Jesus Christ has been there.

From ancient times there has been a perception that certain places hold unique powers for good or evil. Whether these were understood as "sacred groves" or altars dedicated to gods and goddesses, there was coming from the depths of humanity a recognition of the need to set aside places for worship, no matter how skewed and inadequate the religious consciousness that impelled them.

The contemporary fascination with collapsing boundaries of time and space is evidence, perhaps, of a still-unaware longing to know and experience the realization of Christ's astounding bidding at the Last Supper:

> Make your home in me, as I make mine in you.
> As a branch cannot bear fruit all by itself,
> but must remain part of the vine,
> neither can you unless you remain in me....
> If you remain in me
> and my words remain in you,
> you may ask what you will
> and you shall get it....
> Holy Father,
> keep those you have given me true to your name,
> so that they may be one like us....
> I have given them the glory you gave to me,
> that they may be one as we are one.
> With me in them and you in me,
> may they be so completely one
> that the world will realize it was you who sent me.
>   (Jn. 15: 4,7; 17: 11, 22-23)

The meaning of sacred place and space that can be intensely affected (both positively and negatively) by cyberspace has bearing on faith-response to the Holy Eucharist. So many questions through the centuries regarding Eucharistic Presence have centered on the manner in which personal, living Self-Gift is effected through a circle of unleavened bread and a cup of wine that have been transubstantiated into the Body and the Blood, soul and divinity of Jesus Christ. Further, that Presence endures and remains available for adoration and reception in the limited space of a tabernacle. Scoffers question this Real Presence. Space measured in nanometers as well as light years and nuclear energy released with immense intensity do not provide convincing proofs regarding matters of faith, nor explicate the Eucharistic Mystery, but they can offer previously unthinkable analogies for pondering revealed truths.

HUMAN SEXUALITY AND THE VIRTUAL

The living body-person is a sexual person. While this designation, "sexual person," includes physical, anatomical, and hormonal aspects, sexuality encompasses a far greater depth of meaning. Human sexuality is the capacity of the *whole person* to enter into love-giving, life-giving union, in and through the body, in ways that are appropriate to one's state in life.[50] So, whatever influences or actions touch any aspect of the human person, they simultaneously involve that person's sexuality—their capacity for entering into divine and human communion. Indirectly, all aspects of the virtual discussed thus far have bearing on human sexuality.

As noted earlier, Liz Mckenzie explains that *VE's* (virtual environments) projected by a user are predominantly *visual.* This is true not only of advanced forms of *VE.* Visual appa-

---

50.   See Prokes, *Toward a Theology of the Body,* pp. 91-103.

ratus is a feature of many technical instruments in common use today. Palm pilots, wireless phones, portable DVD players and computers have visual components, allowing users to access with immediacy the images of family and associates as well as a countless number of programs. The features of easy visual access coupled with the possibility of private viewing have opened a floodgate of materials (many advertised blatantly through unwanted "Spam" on home computer screens) so that purveyors of pornographic materials may entice viewers. It was recently reported that more people watch pornography than those who watch sportscasts. How did this come about, and what does it mean for those seeking deepened understanding of faith?

While there is no single cause of this relatively new phenomenon, the dramatic and swift "turn to the virtual" is a major element. Other forces include ignorance and misunderstanding of human sexuality; the commercial exploitation of human weakness; faulty education; and the promotion of "easy fixes" for desired pleasure. All of these contribute to the present degradation of lived sexuality.

Underlying much of the commercial sordid portrayal of sex, however, is the turn to the virtual. Recall how Baudrillard cites the loss of correspondence between signs and what they signify, to the extent that a military pilot can return from a bombing mission in a real war and describe his experience as being "like the movies." When there is a rupture between a sign and what it signifies, between a chosen human action and the reality of its meaning and purpose, both the person and the action are diminished and what is acted out can become destructive. Each of the seven levels of virtual reality presented at the beginning of this book has bearing on human sexuality. Their applications in daily life and human relationships can become so familiar and relentless that they seem inevitable and irreversible.

When Pope Paul VI issued *Humanae Vitae*, stating the indissoluble union between love-giving and life-giving, many Catholics opposed it before they had read it, sure that the Pope was out of touch with the state of the world and the new possibilities of preventing birth. It was another "watershed moment" for persons of faith. Either the truths of sexuality and marriage and the genuine freedom they mean are received, or there is a turn to various kinds of "virtual sexuality" and "virtual marriage." Regrettably, those who think it impossible to embrace the unity of love-giving and life-giving are abdicating a basic reality of what it means for them to be a human person. It then becomes easy for purveyors of commercial products to persuade them, as prospective customers, that they cannot control their sexual drive (and possible unwanted consequences) without the aid of commercial devices and pharmaceuticals. The electronic media abound with assurances that it is a civil right to have sexual satisfaction without having to worry about unwanted consequences, or external limitations, civil or religious. To be "free" in a boundaryless world includes the expectation that research will yield more convenient ways of achieving sexual satisfaction.

Creation in the image and likeness of God, however, is the source of human sexual truth and freedom. The full revelation of what it means to live that truth and freedom came in Jesus Christ, who manifested the inner life of God as a Divine Communion of Persons, totally given in mutual loving Self-Gift, and totally receptive to the others. This is forever. Paul VI, addressing particularly the dignity and depth of marital acts, wrote in *Humanae Vitae*: "Conjugal love reveals its true nature and nobility when it is considered in its supreme origin, God, who is love.... Marriage is not, then, the effect of chance or the product of evolution of unconscious natural forces; it is the wise institution of the Creator to realize in mankind His design of love."[51]

There is a chasm between authentic sexual expression in and through the body, and virtual sexual activity, and pleasure is not the determining criterion. Love is. In genuine love there is no artifice or simulation, no substitution or rejection of bodily gift. There is no "avatar" that "stands for" the beloved, no projected environment. It is for real. The act of human intercourse, by its very reality, is a self-gift lived out bodily, a commingling of bodies that by its nature bears the mark of exclusive gift without placing barriers or killing agents in the path of what is being received from the very body-substance of the beloved. This is not a bodily gift that can be indiscriminately given or received "for a price" or for a release of tension, or for brief pleasure. Nor is it a love-act that can be electronically contrived or experienced vicariously. Nor is it a partial gift. These are realities that Pope Paul VI was safeguarding in *Humanae Vitae,* while fully recognizing the exquisite gift of authentic and responsible love.

There is a close link between the principles involved in preparing, eating and drinking in relationship. Every human person is called to eat humanly, and to develop into the fullness of being a truly sexual person. Every celibate person, every single person is called to this fullness in ways that are appropriate to their state of life. If this is misunderstood, or there is simply repression, forms of virtual sexual expression may be very attractive.

Theology must grapple with these issues, aware of scientific and technical insights into the meaning of "space" and "place" and embodiment, discerning what is genuine, and what can prove to be destructive. No longer can there be the luxury of penetrating the great theological texts and history

---

51. Pope Paul VI, *Humanae Vitae: On the Regulation of Birth*, U.S. Catholic Conference Publication No. 280-2 (Washington, DC, July 25, 1968), #1.

of the past without perceiving how they relate to the contemporary experience of faith in a culture that is scientifically and technically operational across all the phases of human life. To understand the lived body as sacred place, as destined for transcendence, ultimately as having the call to be *self-gift* is crucial. Sheldrake writes:

> A catholicity of place is, for Christians, symbolized most powerfully in the *koinonia* of believers filled with the Spirit of Jesus and shaped by Eucharistic "space," which has a particular potency in terms of the tension between local and universal. On the one hand, every Eucharist exists in a particular time and place. On the other hand, each Eucharist is a practice of transgression and a *transitus*, a transit point, a passageway between worlds that prefigures the conclusive "passing over" brought about in death. Eucharistic space enables the particularity of local "place" to intersect in the risen and ascended Jesus with all times and all places.[52]

To substitute illusionary place and space and virtual expressions of body for the profundity of participation in the Mystery of Christ is to lose truth and to invite captivity to technological imagery.

---

52.   Sheldrake, "Human Identity," p. 11.

6

THE VIRTUAL AND THE SUPERNATURAL

Suppose we try to simulate a city full of people. Such simulations are being attempted now, but at a ludicrously inaccurate level.... In principle, we can imagine a simulation being so good that every single *atom* in each person and each object in the city and the properties of each atom has an analogue in the simulation. Let us imagine, in the limit, a simulation that is absolutely perfect.... Furthermore, let us imagine that, when the program is run on some gigantic computer, the temporal evolution of the simulated persons and their city precisely mimics for all time the real temporal evolution of the real people and the real city. An absolutely precise simulation of something is called an *emulation*....

The key question is this: do the emulated people exist? As far as the simulated people can tell, they do. By assumption, any action which the real people can and do carry out to determine whether they exist—reflecting on the fact that they think, interacting with the environment—the emulated people also can do, and in fact do. There is simply no way for the emulated people to tell that they are "really" inside the computer, that they are merely simulated, and not real.[1]

*T*his brief selection from Tipler's book, *The Physics of Immortality*, serves as a cameo for the immense body of issues raised by "the virtual." Tipler explains why he is not a Christian by citing Paul's First Letter to the Corinthians 15:14, where St. Paul says that "if Christ has not been raised, then our preaching is in vain and your faith is in vain." (RSV). I agree with Paul, Tipler avers, saying that it was worth describing at some length *why* he does not believe in the resurrection. He then addresses key aspects of the deposit of faith: the Trinity, transubstantiation, Real Presence in terms of his understanding of The Omega Point, and Deistic Thought.[2] He seeks evidence. That is not new. What is significant here is that Tipler and others such as Ray Kurzweil[3] specifically relate developments in the cyber-world to theological matters. In a particular way, these authors alert theologians to the challenges of the new millennium. They are willing to open issues for dialogue that are not remote, but already require a response.

It was noted earlier that nine scientists, psychologists and theologians, in their cross-discipline book *Whatever Happened to the Human Soul?* present essays that reflect a common conviction that they term "non-reductive physicalism." In their use of this term, "physicalism" represents an agreement with those scientists and philosophers "who hold that it is not necessary to postulate a second metaphysical entity, the soul or mind, to account for human capacities and distinctiveness."[4] On the other hand, the "nonreductive" indi-

---

1.   Frank J. Tipler, *The Physics of Immortality:Modern Cosmology, God and the Resurrection of the Dead* (New York, 1994), pp. 206-207.

2.   See Tipler, *The Physics of Immortality*, pp. 309-327.

3.   See Ray Kurzweil, *The Age of Spiritual Machines* (New York, 1999).

cates their rejection of those contemporary philosophical positions that hold the human person to be "nothing but" a body.[5] They explore what they call the "difficult issue" of maintaining that we *are* our bodies, while acknowledging such human capacities as rationality, free will, emotion, morality, and above all, relationship with God. Thus, according to Nancey Murphy, *nonreductive physicalism* explains the human person as a physical organism "whose complex functioning, both in society and in relation to God, gives rise to 'higher' human capacities such as morality and spirituality."[6]

While Tipler's theory concerning "emulated" people and their capacity to "do whatever real people do" is posited within his more extensive discussion of The Omega Point and its consequences, the quotation introducing this chapter touches upon divine creation, the direct creation of each human soul, the uniqueness of human persons, and free will—indeed, the truth and real existence of the supernatural. If "emulations" are equal to real persons, there is, as he writes, the possibility of emulating the entire universe, providing the computer generating it is big enough. "The dead will be resurrected when the computer capacity of the universe is so large that the amount of capacity required to store all possible human simulations is an insignificant fraction of the entire capacity."[7] Again, there is no attempt in this book to respond to each inter-disciplinary theory or construct regarding aspects of the virtual (something which, in any

---

4.   Warren S. Brown, Nancey Murphy, and H. Newton Malony, *Whatever Happened to the Human Soul?* (Minneapolis, 1998), p. 2.

5.   Ibid.

6.   Murphy, *Whatever Happened to the Human Soul?* p. 25.

7.   Frank J. Tipler, *The Physics of Immortality*, p. 225.

case, is beyond the ability of this author). The purpose is rather to show the multiple ways in which scientific and technological work/theories concerning virtuality implicate matters of faith and the task of theology.

RELEVANCIES FOR THEOLOGY

Revelation does not change, but its renewed explication and application must be addressed and reflected upon in every phase of history. The Second Vatican Council and *The Catechism of the Catholic Church* have brought new clarity of expression to the truths held in Catholic faith, and the principles that constitute a foundation for them have been articulated anew. Yet, there is still a gap between 1) theological expression of Christianity's fundamental truths of faith together with the penetration of their meaning and 2) their applied significance in relating issues that arise from an increasingly virtual environment that is open to confusion concerning what is supernatural and what is merely skillfully projected or emulated in *VR* or *VE*.

Surely the interrelation of the natural and the supernatural is not a novel theological (and philosophical) question, but that relationship becomes increasingly complex at the present time. By the mid-twentieth century, the manner of understanding the supernatural brought sharp debate among Catholic theologians, with Henri deLubac being a particular lightning rod for those who disagreed with him and others of the so-called *nouvelle theologie* school concerning the correct explication of the supernatural. Now, however, it is the very existence of the supernatural that is at issue in the current interplay between the real and the virtual. When the universe and the human person are perceived as completely explicable without reference to the supernatural, there is no need to question the manner in which the natural and the supernatural relate. Similarly, if what currently *seems* inexplicable only requires more highly developed technological means of investigation, the issue of the supernatural fades. On the other hand, every aspect of the *fides quae*, the deposit of faith, depends on the affirmation of the supernatural, opening to ever-deeper penetration in understanding it.

The *Catechism of the Catholic Church* states that the "vocation to eternal life is *supernatural*. It depends entirely on God's gratuitous initiative, for he alone can reveal and give himself. It surpasses the power of human intellect and will, as that of every other creature." (#1998) The supernatural does not refer to what is simply still obscure for human thought and empirical proof—nor does it provide a descriptive label for magic performed according to secret formulae and prescribed gestures. The supernatural, rather, distinguishes the immense realm of truth and reality that exceeds human capacity to perceive, imagine, understand and analyze. As such, supernatural reality includes the very existence of Divine Persons, the divine choice of self-manifestation, the Incarnation and Redemption, efficacious sacramental life, and the call to share eternal life with the Trinity: all clearly involve the existence of the supernatural and can only be received as gratuitous divine gift.

The human person, immersed in an environment that sustains life, receives elements of the outer world through the senses and integrates those aspects that are perceived as good. It is essential for human development that every natural faculty actively responds to sense stimulation, to the capacity to discern and ponder what is perceived as good and true. There are radical limits to these human faculties, however. Either a person will think that the powers to sense, reason, imagine and choose *determine the ultimate horizon of all reality*—or will recognize these faculties as gifts to be transcended by far more radical supernatural gratuities. In the latter case, the outer senses and interior powers provide apt analogies for human openness to participation in supernatural realities that exceed their ability to fathom, measure and control.

It is here precisely that issues discussed in previous chapters concerning genuine boundaries, honest interface, and receptivity to divine initiatives require a recognition of the supernatural. The truths concerning them depend upon the difference between divine *gift* and human *acquisition*. A genuine gift has the following characteristics:

- It is totally gratuitous, given in freedom.
- It is bestowed person to person.
- It cannot be required, specified, earned, or demanded as a right.
- It is not contrived, but bears the element of surprise and the unexpected.
- A gift expresses love and relationship.
- It is appropriate for the person and the occasion.

Acquisitions, on the other hand, have the following characteristics:

- Acquiring often requires human effort and planning.
- While it may involve persons, it focuses on an agreement, perhaps an exchange value.
- It can be earned, or demanded as a rightful gain.
- Acquisitions can involve planning, negotiation, and usually lack the element of surprise.
- Acquisition can belongs to the economic as well as the personal realm.
- Decisions concerning an acquisition's appropriateness are often part of a transaction.

Participation in the mysteries of faith is received as divine gift and is characterized in terms of authentic gift. The technical capacity to fabricate and/or interact with what is virtual, on the other hand, belongs to the realm of acquisitions. This is not to deny the goodness of acquisitions in general. They are necessary in conducting affairs of life. Distinguishing *gift* from *acquisition* here, however, sheds light on the necessary distinction between what is supernatural and what is virtual. Unless the distinction is clear, the simply "virtual" can be misunderstood as 1) replacing what was formerly thought to be supernatural beings or powers; 2) obviating any perceived need for what is supernatural; or 3) creating virtual universes (perhaps perfect emulations) "peopled" with virtual beings of one's making and unmaking. Such misunderstandings can bring confusion regarding Divine Revelation and the truths of faith, or evoke disdain for the latter in light of the human capacity to concoct imaginative worlds. The mysteries of faith and the reality of personal relationship with divine Persons are in the domain of *gift* and involve what is supernatural.

Divine Revelation has made known the existence of the supernatural—which can only be received as gift, and is not humanly contrived. The supernatural, which surpasses human inventiveness, extends to the limitless realities of divine existence and gratuitous divine creativity. St. Paul wrote of "what eye has not seen and ear has not heard," and The Nicene Creed affirms God as creator of all that is "seen and unseen." The projection of virtual worlds and the human penetration of the interface between what is real and what is virtual (as technically brilliant as these may be) are all combinations of images, phenomena, and technique that remain within the orbit of the humanly conceived, imagined, and fabricated. They are acquisitions of human mind and creativity, and remain enclosed within the human ambit.

Note that the distinction being made here is not between the *natural* and the *supernatural*. Rather a distinction is drawn here *between the supernatural* and *that which is able to be accommodated by human intellect and will*. So, in regard to the supernatural, the core issue in this present work is the need for clarity regarding the difference between what is a product of human ingenuity in the fashioning of what is virtual, and what is divinely, gratuitously given.

In an essay linking the film *The Matrix Reloaded* to the present state of American life, Hank Stuever appeals to Plato's allegory of the cave:

> Do we exist as we think we do? Is life a lie? Can we somehow unplug from this reality and find salvation in the real reality? ... Hopelessly bound to the infotainment machine, waistlines sprawling, thumbs sore from video games, we ache for the physical movement that has become the trademark of "Matrix" living.
>
> People now daydream in rotoscopic slow motion, with a pulsing techno beat soundtrack. You see it sometimes in how they handle their cell phones.... There's this vague vibe that our modern lives are really all just some predetermined, exquisitely programmed matrix. We've watched too many car commercials, earned too many liberal arts degrees, gone to the movies too much, read too many comic books, possessed too much shiny metal. This will be our characteristic pose in the history books: sullen, dystopian, jaded. All clad in black, with flecks of neon green here and there, living in a fantasy made solely of stuff we saw reflected on the cave wall.[8]

---

8. Hank Stuever, "A 'Matrix'-Loaded Universe's Daydream Reality," in *The Washington Post*, C1 and C5, July 2003.

Stuever's questions and societal commentary deal with uncertain boundaries, shadows of reality, and a dark futility that is not silenced, but fed by immersion in a vibrating, image-laden culture. There is no sense of fulfillment, but a sense of being caught in a ceaseless surge of activity that is part real, part merely shadowy projection. Stuever suggests as much: he reflects on the devotees of other film series whom he labels "Lucasites," "Tolkienists," "Fans of the X-Men," and "The Harry Potter children":

> So this powerful identification with the idea of a matrix is perhaps merely a coping mechanism. It's one more fantasy that makes the reality more real. It gets you through those days where you don't know what to believe.
>
> Before the movie [*The Matrix Reloaded*] started, while people were still talking on their phones and unwrapping contraband food-court nosh, a commercial came on featuring the evil Agent Smith. He told us to drink Powerade thirst quencher.
>
> There was this creepy vibe in the air that we'd already drunk it, swallowed very drop, plugged in to such a degree that we never escape.[9]

Stuever's essay underscores the challenges that accompany transmigration between fantasy worlds and the ordinary, but often daunting, realities of embodied daily life. He portrays a cultural phenomenon that might be termed neo-shadow-watchers in the cinematic cave, who drink not only of the projections on the screen, but also the advice of imaginary characters. The effect is too often a jadedness that "gets

---

9.   Stuever, "A 'Matrix'-Loaded Universe's Daydream Reality," C5.

you through the days where you don't know what to believe."

Why do so many find a strong appeal in films such as *The Matrix*? Steve Kellmeyer attributes the appeal to quasi-Christian themes woven into the plot, to themes that have a Gnostic base. He maintains that *The Matrix* gives a Gnostic version of salvation history. The names of characters (e.g. Neo, Trinity, and Morpheus) are not subtle, and the water-baptismal symbolism is pervasive.[10] There are themes of Call, the New Adam, the Last Supper, Passion, Descent into Death/Hell, and Resurrection.

The meaning of the supernatural does not directly emerge in Stuever's *Matrix*-centered essay, but the hollow-ness left when it is absent is evident. Is it the supernatural undertow, pulling insistently at the core of the human per-son that, despite resistance to it, draws many to the virtual? In the realm of acquisition where the virtual is located, there is a sense of being in control, of deciding how desires may be fulfilled, of changing scenarios and relationships at will in a pseudo-universe of one's own making. Yet, there is a certain openness to risk, to the unknown, and a willingness to be influenced and even controlled by what lies behind the inter-face.

GIFT: THE FIRST CATEGORY OF BEING

Gift excludes control. In an earlier work I propose that *gift* is not only a prime characteristic of Christian faith—it is the foundational characteristic of Trinitarian personal life, and of all reality. It is neither process nor substance that is the first category of Being or Existence, but Person-Gift.[11] In

---

10.   See Kellmeyer, "The New Gnostic Gospel," in *Envoy*, p. 37.

the Last Discourse, Jesus described the perichoretic life of the one God as a communion of persons, whose identity is that of *relation*: of Person-Gift poured out to each of the other Divine Persons and totally receptive of them. All created reality has vestiges of the Trinity in some way, but human persons bear the Trinitarian image and likeness as their most fundamental identity. That is why, when there is only a simulation of *gift*, it is destructive of persons and relationships.

In any theological grappling with the issues presented by virtual reality, growing understanding of *gift* will have a particular relevance. So many contemporary moral issues commence here. The prime basis of all gifts is a supernatural reality: the inner life of the Trinity. It cannot be contrived, or be replaced by what is contrived. The longing for all that is meant by *gift* as the most primordial of all reality, however, can *seem* to be at least assuaged, if not fulfilled, by what is only imitation, simulation, and/or full-body immersion in the virtual.

Since so much of life in Western cultures is already deeply immersed in what is virtual, its applications in human life are taken for granted in ways that earlier generations would not have envisioned. It is the effects of this immersion on ordinary perceptions of reality and responsibility that significantly affect the task of moral theology at the present time. The current ambiguity in use of terms that once had a common meaning is but one indication of the difficulty of the task. Words such as "sacramental," "marriage," and "family," for example, no longer have common referents in real life because they are applied according to individual interpretations, and used to defend lifestyles and modes of conduct considered contradictory to them several decades ago. Pope

---

11.   See Mary Timothy Prokes, *Mutuality: The Human Image of Trinitarian Love* (New York, 1993), pp. 27-30.

John Paul II, in his encyclical *Veritatis Splendor,* succinctly showed why teleological and proportionalist theories fail in clarifying moral issues, since they obfuscate the true meaning of a human moral act. He points out "The primary and decisive element for moral judgment is the object of the human act, which establishes whether it is *capable of being ordered to the good and to the ultimate end, which is God.* This capability is grasped by reason in the very being of man, considered in his integral truth, and therefore in his natural inclinations, his motivations, and his finalities, which always have a spiritual dimension as well."[12] If, however, there is ambiguity about the meaning of integral truth, natural inclinations and finalities, it is not possible to *reason* authentically and to search communally for applications to basic issues of moral life. Such reasoning depends upon a common understanding of terms. When seeking an understanding of faith (the encompassing theological task) there must be some agreement regarding the meaning of core words as the struggles of early Ecumenical Councils confirm and exemplify.

Confusion is rife regarding supernatural realities. This is surely not a new issue within the human family. The media are saturated with words and images associated with the Scriptures, Christianity, and eschatology. Perhaps no word is more frequently applied to economic and medical pursuits than "miracle," and special effects give the illusion of supernatural occurrences and beings.

Theology needs to reclaim and reconfirm the authentic meaning of basic terms and images concerning supernatural truths. Hans Urs von Balthasar pointed out: "All external scenes of Jesus' life and sufferings are to be understood as a direct revelation of the interior life and intentions of God. This is the fundamental meaning of biblical symbolism and

---

12.   Veritatis Splendor, #79.

allegory, without which the whole Gospel remains nothing but superficial moralism."[13] From the silence of Jesus before Caiphas, to the flogging, the nailing to the cross, the piercing of His heart and His final words from the cross, "All is a direct portrayal and exegesis of God (Jn. 1:18) accessible to the senses."[14]

In order for personal, divine supernatural realities to touch human life efficaciously, and enable receptivity to that which exceeds the human capacity to reason, analyze, and duplicate, there must be a way of mediating the interior life and intentions of God. Jesus Christ *is* the encounter point, as von Balthasar's words emphasize. This is Catholic faith at its heart, expressed throughout the canon of the New Testament, wrestled after great suffering into dogmatic expression at Councils, celebrated in every liturgy and manifest in the living witness of the saints. The question is: how are the mysteries of faith to be newly penetrated in the Holy Spirit and newly expressed in the opening years of the Third Millennium? Numerical turning points, such as the Millennium, invite fresh speculation. The monumental year 2000 was marked, both within Christianity as "the Year of Our Lord," and by members of "New Age" groups as the "Dawning of the Age of Aquarius." The beginning of the new millennium is an interface moment between faith/theology and those who seek fulfillment in Aquarian teaching and practices.

On February 3, 2003, the Pontifical Councils for Culture and Interreligious Dialogue issued a substantive document entitled *Jesus Christ, the Bearer of the Water of Life: A Christian Reflection on the New Age.* The writers of the docu-

---

13.   Hans Urs von Balthasar, *The Grain of Wheat: Aphorisms* (San Francisco, 1995), p. 58.

14.   Ibid.

ment stated that "The study is a provisional report,"[15] intended as a guide for Catholics in preaching the Gospel and teaching the faith, not providing answers to all questions raised by adherents of the New Age, but recognizing that they express contemporary "signs" of the enduring human search for happiness, meaning and salvation. Astrologers believe that the "Age of Pisces," which is described as the "Christian Age," is now giving way to the Age of Aquarius, which according to the lyrics of a song from the Broadway musical *Hair*, will be a time of harmony and understanding:

> When the Moon is in the Seventh House, and Jupiter aligns with Mars, then Peace will guide the Planets, and Love will steer the Stars. This is the dawning of the Age of Aquarius.... Harmony and understanding, sympathy and trust abounding; no more falsehoods or derision—golden living , dreams of visions, mystic crystal revelation and the mind's true liberation. Aquarius.[16]

The name "New Age" encompasses a number of different characteristics, and the document from the Pontifical Councils notes that adherents have a marked preference for Eastern or pre-Christian religions, ancient agricultural rites and fertility cults, with Gaia or Mother Earth seen as alternative to God the Father. In New Age literature, Jesus Christ is often treated as "one among many wise men or initiates or avatars" (#4.) Since Jesus is not considered the "only" Christ, His death on the cross is denied or reinterpreted, excluding the notion that a "Christ" could suffer, and extrabiblical

---

15. Pontifical Councils for Culture and Interreligious Dialogue, *Jesus Christ, the Bearer of the Water of Life: A Christian Reflection on the New Age*, in *Origins*, CNS Documentary Service, 32, No.35 (February 13, 2000), Foreword, p. 570.

16. See Notes to *Jesus Christ, the Bearer of the Water of Life*, #20.

writings such as the neo-Gnostic Gospels are perceived as more authentic than the canonical Gospels regarding Jesus. Among the questions that writers of the Pontifical Councils' document place in order to provide a key to New Age thought is one that directly relates to "the virtual." They ask regarding "the human being" if there is only one universal being or many individuals. In answer to this question, they appeal to the work of Michel Lacroix, who wrote:

> The point of New Age techniques is to reproduce mystical states at will, as if it were a matter of laboratory material. Rebirth, biofeedback, sensory isolation, holotropic breathing, hypnosis, mantras, fasting, sleep deprivation and transcendental meditation are attempts to control these states and to experience them continuously.[17]

There is a definite appeal of the virtual in New Age practices. Among these practices is "channeling," or the claimed ability of psychic mediums to gain information from "other selves, usually disembodied entities living on a higher plane." Channeling "links beings as diverse as ascended masters, angels, gods, group entities, nature spirits and the higher self."[18] What is manifest in the surge toward New Age beliefs and practices (an amalgam which includes elements of ancient and Eastern religions, Judaism, Christianity, astrology, and the occult) is the desire to overcome boundaries, to find an interconnected energy. It expresses a human desire for privileged knowledge and union, a self-fulfillment

---

17.   See *Jesus Christ, the Bearer of the Water of Life*, #4, and Note 70, citing Michael Lacroix, *L'Ideologia della New Age* (Milan, 1998), p. 74.

18.   *Jesus Christ, Bearer of the Water of Life*, Glossary.

that can be termed neo-Gnostic, and answers the human hunger for ritual.

Ultimately, the New Age is expressing a longing for the authentically supernatural, redolent of the outcry of St. Augustine in his *Confessions*, who described so vividly what it meant to seek it fruitlessly in Manichaeism, an outgrowth of Gnosticism.

Perhaps *interface* is one of the most significant terms needing to be probed and brought into new theological meaning at this time of search, when there rises in humanity a new longing for transcendence. The word "interface" can mean simply the screen on which an image appears. Much more, it can designate a place of encounter, of interchange. What the developers of virtual reality indicate by "interface" carries a virtual meaning, but what *interface* might mean if recognized as a definite theological term remains to be developed. This could prove to be a positive gift emerging from the press toward the virtual.

In poetry and songs of love, the face is extolled as conveying personal identity, of being a vulnerable expression of the interior person, particularly through the eyes. Lovers desire to gaze into one another's eyes. To be face-to-face is an intimate encounter and the Church has always treasured the meaning of eternal life in terms of seeing God face-to-face. *Interface*, however, can indicate something more radical—a compenetration of intimate presence and knowledge, a true crossing-over into the other at a point of vulnerability. Analogically, it carries resonances of perichoretic indwelling and compenetration. Is this the deeper longing that is being unconsciously sought by those who are drawn to the simulated crossing-over that occurs between person and instrument at the interface screen in advanced forms of virtual reality?

7

Theological Implications for the New Millennium

*A*t the outset of this work it was asserted without hesitation that no other "sign of the times" requires greater attention of the Church and contemporary theologians than the rapidly developing complexity summarized in the term *Virtual Reality.* The ensuing chapters addressed specific levels and characteristics of "the virtual" that now inundate daily life in the so-called developed countries of the world.

In citing the virtual as focus for theological study and insight it is necessary to emphasize several things:

1. There is no suggestion here of returning to a "pre-virtual reality" period. All authentic theology takes place within a given historical moment and must take into account, as John Macquarrie emphasized, not only revelation, Scripture and tradition, but also experience, culture, and reason.[1] Perceptive reading of "the signs of the times" is a vital aspect of responsible theologizing.

2. Theological wisdom will recognize that major eruptions of new thought, creativity, and human endeavor occur in

a cosmos held within Divine Providence, even if their
initial expressions are flawed—or even perverse. In
Christ, it must be asked: what good, what truth is
emerging in these new pursuits that needs to be recognized and brought into the patterns of Redemption?

It is in that light that the multiple forms of virtual reality
need to be dealt with seriously in terms of faith and its
understanding. Although a number of theological issues have
been raised in the previous chapters, it seems important to
focus also on several other matters which are particularly apt
for consideration, since they hold an important twofold
aspect: 1) the potential for greater theological investigation
and explication, or 2) the potential for destructive patterns
in regard to Christian faith and human life generally.

There is need to ponder, at root, *why* the virtual presently bears such fascination and exercises such intense
absorptive power over contemporary humanity. I write the
concluding pages of this book a brief time after returning
from teaching a theology course in Cameroon, West Africa.
For millions of Cameroonians, even the rudimentary means
of electronic communication are scarce. The availability of
dependable electric power and potable running water and
rudimentary protection from disease are still uncommon in
this country blessed with numerous natural resources. It will
be some time before the realities of daily life in that nation
are overrun by electronic virtuality. Yet, in a globally condensed world, the effects of virtual patterns already penetrate
this land. Patrons of Air France, for example, traveling in and
out of Douala, Cameroon's major port city, could see on the

---

1.   See John Macquarrie, *Principles of Christian Theology*, 2nd ed.
      (New York, 1977), pp. 4-18.

back cover of Air France's magazine-of-the-month, the photo of a woman in seductive pose together with a neo-Cartesian assertion: "I sense. Therefore I am." The juxtaposition of daily life and the advertisement is symptomatic of the fragmentation and disjuncture that are so pervasive of society at the present time. Beneath both the authentic cry of a Cameroonian boy hawking pineapples along a red clay road, and the deviant, sophisticated commerce across a woman's image, there is the insistent human longing to communicate, even somehow to tap into the "marvelous exchange" wrought in the Incarnation. Major hallmarks of the present age are instant communication, extravagant amounts of information, and the longing for immediate interaction. To a large extent these remain at the level of the *virtual* in so-called developed nations.

With new intensity the Church in recent years speaks, writes, evangelizes in terms of *Communion of Persons*. Christ's Last Discourse is brought to new awareness at this moment of history:

> To have seen me is to have seen the Father,
> so how can you say, "Let us see the Father"?
> Do you not believe
> that I am in the Father and the Father is in me?
> The words I say to you I do not speak as from myself:
> it is the Father, living in me, who is doing this work.
> You must believe me when I say
> that I am in the Father and the Father is in me.
> (Jn. 14: 9-11)

> May they all be one.
> Father, may they be one in us,
> as you are in me and I am in you,
> so that the world will believe it was you who sent me.
> (Jn. 17:21)

This prayer of Christ is a touchstone for probing what is positive in the contemporary possibilities of electronic communication and interchange. A range of questions emerges here. What does it mean now that Christ prays for the possibility of "living within one another" in the human image of Trinitarian relations? What is the potential for that living within one another presently—not virtually, but in truth? From what has been learned of material reality, including the human body and the constant interchange among material bodies in the cosmos, what is this saying in relation to Christ's prayer? What is it saying of the Eucharist, the reception of Holy Communion, and Real Presence?

These are not obvious, indifferent questions. At a time when bodiliness and genuine presence seem unimportant (or easily interchangeable) in light of electronic simulations, it is crucial that persons of faith understand more deeply why there is a precious uniqueness to each person's body as outward expression/presence of the person.

Currently, as discussed in an earlier chapter, there is the desire to "cross over" into artificial environments in order to interact with avatars of one's own or another's making. What import does the contrived projection of pseudo-beings have in terms of replacing real relationships? More deeply, how does the fabrication of virtual beings touch upon the fabrication of human life and other life forms in the laboratories of the Western world? With the proliferation of experimentation regarding the uses of DNA, stem cells, and body parts, when will there be such a radical departure from what is clearly human that creatures of human making will have no capacity to be recognized as belonging to the human race for which the Second Person of the Blessed Trinity became man, lived, suffered, died and rose, and is Eucharistically present? *There is no such thing as an "artificial person."* Who or what will such creations be? These are not frivolous questions.

Some have been raised before, but never with the same need for intense, direct theological reflection.

What is vital, however, is to probe *why* there is a craving to fabricate human life forms and radically change what it means to be human. What might this prompt, or what can it open so that the Holy Spirit can lead to greater understanding of the fullness of truth concerning humanity? In Augustine's era, it was the serious matters surrounding salvation that prodded his explication of grace. In our own time, the rush to technical development of the virtual is also prodding theologians to ask more deeply than ever before: What does it mean to be human? To be the image of God? What are the parameters of the human? What are the limits for altering the human body? How lay deeper foundations for understanding the meaning of genetic inheritance, of *continuity* in the human family? What does it mean to be present?

Surely one of the anomalies of virtual communication is that it isolates and disembodies even as it allows interchange on a simulated level. In telephone communications, what seems to be a familiar voice with recognizable intonations, is actually an electronic signal, passed along wires or conveyed wirelessly. How can theological exploration of such communication *open the questions* of prayer, of communion with the saints and those who have died in God's friendship? Or communication with the angels? There is great need to ponder this from the aspect of applied theology. For millennia, people have sought to contact deceased family members through séances or cultic practices. More recently, some New Age adepts promise contact with the dead through the help of "guides." How adequate is present Catholic theology concerning communion with those who have died? How is this to be clearly differentiated from simulated interaction with avatars?

It is apparent that theologians need to explore and explicate the significance of *continuity* and coinherence among the truths of faith. Every mystery of faith involves continuity and enduring fidelity. What will theology in the Third Millennium contribute in this regard? In virtual environments, constant, pulsing change is prized. Contemporary society tends to disdain that which "has been" as narrow, and no longer relevant at the cutting-edge of the future. To break loose from what was formerly considered enduring, and to venture boldly into what was formerly forbidden seem for many to be marks of the heroic, self-made individual: beholden to no creed, cult, or permanent commitment. To scorn enduring realities and to cut loose from the roots that have nourished Church, society, and culture is to invite illusion of freedom. The statement of "openly gay" Reverend V. Gene Robinson, after the Episcopal General Convention confirmed his election to be consecrated bishop of New Hampshire, succinctly expresses this. In a news conference that followed the Episcopal vote, Robinson acknowledged that some opposed his election as bishop because of traditional church teaching on homosexuality. He then said: *"Just simply to say that it goes against tradition and the teaching of the church and Scripture does not necessarily make it wrong."*[2] From within Christian congregations it becomes increasingly facile to dismiss continuity with the roots of faith while maintaining convenient titles and labels.

Kay Itoi, in a *Newsweek* magazine special issue on inventions, described "optical camouflage." This technology would allow both the capacity to see through solid objects (such as the floor of an airplane cockpit), or alternatively, the ability to hide what is actually present by means of "an invisibility cloak." The invention would make "virtual windows"

---

2.   Alan Cooperman, "Episcopal Church Confirms Gay Bishop," in *The Washington Post* (August 6, 2003), A5.

possible. "Soon it may be harder than ever to know what's real and what isn't," writes Itoi.[3]

Such altering of perceptions of physical realities in the near-environment touches not only bodily reality and presence, but the meaning of sacramental life. Sacraments are for the living, the embodied. They require real presence on the part of the minister and recipients(s) when there is an *ex opere operato* administration of the sacrament. Sacraments involve the use of specific matter such as unleavened bread, grape wine, blessed oils and water, each having a definite significance. The words and specific matter are at one in the administering of the sacrament—they are actual, not open to substitution or only "apparent" reality. How crucial it is that theological reflection on the sacraments takes into account the ways that substitutions, "appearances," and non-reality already characterize so much of daily life.

Accepting the reality of Jesus' self-gift in the Body and the Blood became the watershed choice for his disciples. When the crowds sought Him after being fed abundantly, Jesus spoke of the Bread that was His own self-gift. "My flesh is real food and my blood is real drink," He assured them, and it was on that point of reality that most of his followers left Him.

Again, two millennia later, it is the question of reality that becomes a watershed for the Church and for humanity. It will not do to wring hands over the inadequacies of an increasingly virtual world, or simply to speak jeremiads to a generation swirling in high-speed, ever-changing virtual experiences. Beneath and through all of this there is the unrecognized cry of the heart for what is authentic, open to eternal love and relationship. Already in 1957, Giovanni

---

3.   Kay Itoi, "Disappearing Act," in *Newsweek* (June 30, 2003 / July 7, 2003, CXLI, No. 26 and CXLII, No. 1), p. 64.

Battista Montini, later Pope Paul VI, wrote a pastoral letter to the Ambrosian Diocese on *Man's Religious Sense*. Prophetically, Montini summarized disjunctures that needed to be addressed:

> Modern man has neglected the study of "being" in itself and of the human soul; he has confined himself to external phenomena and psychological experiences. He no longer concerns himself with his angelic but innate capacity to reach out to something beyond the realm of natural experience, with his unquenchable urge to pass beyond the frontiers of the finite world, with the elementary necessity that constrains him to derive his logical processes, even those governing the positive sciences, from an Absolute, a Necessity. And this is what lies behind all the tragedies—spiritual, cultural, social, political—of the world today as it spins its giddy course devoid of the central axis of security, order and peace.[4]

There is an insistent human longing for *Communion*, the image of Trinitarian life, that is rising up within humanity at the present time, but is constantly in danger of being trapped in what is pseudo-fulfillment. Joseph Cardinal Ratzinger underscores the startling reality of Eucharistic Communion: When the Mystery is received in the fullness of truth, it is the authentic realization of desires that throb in contemporary forays into the virtual:

> It is truly the one, identical Lord, whom we receive in the Eucharist, or better, the Lord who receives us and assumes us into himself. St. Augustine expressed this in a short passage which he perceived as a sort of vision: eat

---

4. Giovanni Battista Montini, *Man's Religious Sense: A Pastoral Letter to the Ambrosian Diocese*, (Westminster, MD, 1957), p. 23.

the bread of the strong; you will not transform me into yourself, but I will transform you into me. In other words, when we consume bodily nourishment, it is assimilated by the body, becoming itself a part of ourselves. But this bread is of another type. It is greater and higher than we are. It is not we who assimilate it, but it assimilates us to itself, so that we become in a certain way "conformed to Christ," as Paul says, members of his body, one in him.

We all "eat" *the same person*, not only the same thing; we are all in this way taken out of our closed individual persons and placed inside another, greater one. We are all assimilated into Christ and so by means of communion with Christ, united among ourselves, rendered the same, one sole thing in him, members of one another.[5]

The task of theology at the beginning of the Third Millennium is clear: the explication of the profound gifts of the faith, received at ever-greater depth, enriched by interdisciplinary insights, but keenly alert to the most pervasive "sign of the times"—virtual reality.

---

5.   Joseph Cardinal Ratzinger, *Eucharist, Communion and Solidarity*, Lecture at the Bishops' Conference of the Region of Campania in Benevento (Italy), June 2, 2002.

INDEX

BIBLIOGRAPHY

Achenbach, Joel. "FUTURE Perfect: Your house is about to get very smart. Ready?" *The Washington Post*, October 8, 1999, H1 and H16-17.

Anderson, Ray S. "On Being Human: The Spiritual Saga of a Creaturely Soul." In *Whatever Happened to the Soul? Scientific and Theological Portraits of Human Nature.* Warren S. Brown, Nancey Murphy and H. Newton Maloney eds. Minneapolis, MN: Fortress Press, 1998, pp. 177-194.

Ashley, Benedict. *Theologies of the Body: Humanist and Christian.* Braintree, MA: The Pope John Center, 1985.

Bauer, Esther M. "An Impulse to Happiness." *The Washington Post*, March 28, 2000, Health: p. 8.

Brueggemann, Walter. *The Land: Place as Gift, Promise and Challenge in Biblical Faith.* Philadelphia, PA: Fortress, 1977.

Brungs, Robert. *You See Lights Breaking Upon Us: Doctrinal Perspectives on Biological Advance.* St. Louis, MO: Versa Press, 1989.

Catechism of the Catholic Church. Second ed. Vatican City: Libreria Vaticana, 1997.

Considering Veritatis Splendor. John Wilkins, ed. Cleveland, OH: The Pilgrim Press, 1994.

Cooperman, Alan. "Episcopal Church Confirms Gay Bishop." *The Washington Post*, August 6, 2003, p. A1, A5.

Dei Verbum: Dogmatic Constitution on Divine Revelation. In *Vatican Council II: The Conciliar and Post Conciliar Documents*, new revised ed. Austin Flannery, gen. ed. Grand Rapids, MI: William B. Eerdmans Publishing Co., 1992, pp. 750-765.

"Eating disorders: Obesity, Bulimia, and Anorexia, A Cultural Epidemic." Information bulletin prepared for Governor's Drug Free Communities Grants Program. See http://www.naples.net/social/jft0001.htm.

Freydis. See counterorder.com. Last upgraded September, 2002.

Garreau, Joel. "The Next Generation: Biotechnology May Make Superhero Fantasy a Reality." *The Washington Post*, April 26, 2002, pp. C1 and C4.

Gates, Bill. "Will Frankenfood Feed the World?" *Time*, 155, No. 25 (June 19,2000): 78-79.

Gaudium et Spes. In *Vatican Council II: The Conciliar and Post Conciliar Documents*, new rev. ed. Austin Flannery, gen. ed. Grand Rapids, MI: William B. Eerdmans Publishing Co., 1992, pp. 903-1001.

"Genetics: Where Do We Draw the Line?" *Beijing Review* (Communist Party Weekly), July 24, 2000. In *World Press Review*, November 2000, p. 41.

Goulder, Michael, "Jesus, the Man of Universal Destiny." In *The Myth of God Incarnate*, John Hick, ed. Philadelphia, PA: The Westminster Press, 1977, pp. 48-63.

Guardini, Romano. *The End of the Modern World.* Wilmington, DE: The Newman Press, 1998.

Guissani, Luigi. *Exercises of the Fraternity of Communion and Liberation: The Miracle of Change.* Rimini, 1998.

Hayles, N. Katherine. *How We Became Posthuman: Virtual Bodies in Cybernetics, Literature, and Informatics.* Chicago: The University of Chicago Press, 1999.

_____. "Virtual Bodies and Flickering Images." In *October*, 66 (Fall).

Heim, Michael. *The Metaphysics of Virtual Reality.* New York: Oxford University Press, 1993.

Hillis, Ken. *Digital Sensations.* Minneapolis, MN: University of Minnesota Press, 1999.

Itoi, Kay. "Disappearing Act." *Newsweek*, CXLI, No. 26 and CXLII, No. 1 (June 30 and July 7, 2003): 64.

Jerusalem Bible, The. Alexander Jones et al, eds. Garden City, NY: Doubleday and Co., 1966.

John Paul II, Pope. *Ecclesia de Eucharistia*, Encyclical. Rome: St. Peter's, April 17, 2003.

_____. *Veritatis Splendor*, Encyclical. Rome: Saint Peter's, August 6, 1993.

Jones, Stephen. "Towards a Philosophy of Virtual Reality." A paper reviewing the first "Consciousness Reframed Conference" at the Centre for Advanced Inquiry into the Interactive Arts, University of Wales, July 1997.

Kass, Leon. *Life, Liberty and the Defense of Dignity: The Challenge for Bioethics.* San Francisco, CA: Encounter Books, 2002.

_____. *Toward a More Natural Science: Biology and Human Affairs.* New York: The Free Press, 1985.

Keillor, Garrison. "In Search of Lake Wobegon." *National Geographic*, 200, No. 12 (December 2000): 87-109.

Kellmeyer, Steve. "The New Gnostic Gospel," *Envoy, 4,* No. 5, pp. 34-39.

Kelly, J. N. D. *Early Christian Doctrines*, rev. ed. New York: Harper and Row, 1978.

Kunzru, Hari. "You Are Cyborg." In *Wired Digital, Inc.* Issue 5:02, February 1997.

Kurzweil, Ray. *The Age of Spiritual Machines.* New York: Viking Press, 1999.

Lacroix, Michael. *L'Ideologia della New Age.* Milan: Il Saggiatore, 1998.

Lanier, Jaron, and Frank Biocca. "An Insider's View of the Future of Virtual Reality." *Journal of Communications,* 42, No. 4 (1992): 150-172.

Leeming, Bernard. *Principles of Sacramental Theology,* 2nd ed. Westminster, MD: The Newman Press, 1960.

Magnificat 4, No. 5. Spencerville, MD (July 2002).

Macquarrie, John. *Principles of Christian Theology,* 2nd ed. New York: Charles Scribner's Sons, 1977.

Maguire, G. Q. and Ellen M. McGee. "Implantable Brain Chips? Time for Debate." *The Hastings Center Report* (January-February, 1999): 7-13.

"Media Guide to the Human Genome Project." Site sponsored by U. S. Department of Energy Office of Science, Office of Biological and Environmental Research, Human Genome Project: http://www.ornl.gov/hgmis/resource/media.html.

Merton, Thomas. *Thoughts in Solitude.* Boston, MA: Shambhala, 1993.

Mizrach, Steve. "Should there be a limit placed on the integration of humans and computers and electronic technology?" See http://www.limmat.ch/koni/texte/cyborg-ethics.html.

Montini, Giovanni Battista. *Man's Religious Sense: A Pastoral Letter to the Ambrosian Diocese.* Westminster, MD: The Newman Press, 1957.

More, Thomas. *Care of the Soul: A Guide for Cultivating Depth and Sacredness in Everyday Life.* New York: Harper Collins Publishers, 1992.

Morse, Margaret. "What Do Cyborgs Eat? Oral Logic in an Information Society." In *Culture on the Brink: Ideologies of Technology.* Gretchen Bender and Timothy Druckrey, eds. Dia Center for the Arts, No. 9. Seattle, WA: Bay Press, 1994.

Murphy, Nancey. "Human Nature: Historical, Scientific, and Religious Issues." In *Whatever Happened to the*

Human Soul? Scientific and Theological Portraits of Human Nature. Warren S. Brown, Nancey Murphy and H. Newton Maloney, eds. Minneapolis, MN: Fortress Press, 1998, pp. 1-29.

Paul VI, Pope. *Humanae Vitae*: On the Regulation of Birth. U. S. Catholic Conference Publication No. 280-2. Washington, DC, July 25, 1968.

"Poor Chinese Selling Their Body Parts, Report Says." Hong Kong (October 30, 2000). ZENIT.org. ZE00103022.

Pontifical Councils for Culture and Interreligious Dialogue, *Jesus Christ, the Bearer of the Water of Life: A Christian Reflection on the New Age*, in *Origins* CNS documentary Service, 32, No. 35, February 13, 2003.

"Project Cyborg 1.0." See http://www.rdg.ac.uk/KevinWarwick/html/project-cyborg-1-0.html.

Prokes, Mary Timothy. *Mutuality: The Human Image of Trinitarian Love*. New York: Paulist Press, 1993.

_____. *Toward a Theology of the Body*. Grand Rapids, MI: William B. Eerdmans Publishing Company, 1996.

Rahner, Karl. *Theological Investigations IV.* Kevin Smyth, trans. Baltimore, MD: Helicon Press, 1966.

Ratzinger, Joseph Cardinal. *Eucharist, Communion and Solidarity.* Lecture at the Bishops' Conference of the Region of Compania, Benevento, Italy, June 2, 2002.

Ryan, Marie-Laure. *Narrative as Virtual Reality: Immersion and Interactivity in Literature and Electronic Media.* Baltimore, MD: The Johns Hopkins University Press, 2001.

Sawyer, Kathy. "Unveiling the Universe." *National Geographic*, 196, No. 4 (October 1999): 8-25, 32-41.

Schettler, Renee. "A Feast with Fewer Carbs Than a Slice of Pumpkin Pie." *The Washington Post*, November 19, 2003, F1, F9.

Sheehan, Archbishop Michael J. "Is the Eucharist Really Christ's Body and Blood?" Letter. See http://www.petersnet.net/browse/1340.htm.

Sheldrake, Philip. "Human Identity and the Particularity of Place." *Spiritus: A Journal of Christian Spirituality*, I, No. 1 (2000): 43-64.

Stuever, Hank. "A 'Matrix'-Loaded Universe's Daydream Reality." *The Washington Post*, July 2003, C1 and C5.

Tipler, Frank, Jr. *The Physics of Immortality*. New York: Doubleday, 1994.

Tertullian. *De Carne Christi*. Ernest Evans trans. London: SPCK, 1965.

Vagaggini, Cipriano. *The Flesh: Instrument of Salvation: A Theology of the Human Body*. Staten Island, NY: Alba House, 1969.

Vatican Council II: The Conciliar and Post Conciliar Documents. Second ed. Austin Flannery gen. ed. Grand Rapids, MI: William B. Eerdmans Publishing Co., 1992.

Vogel, Arthur. *Body Theology: God's Presence in Man's World*. New York: Harper and Row, 1973.

Von Balthasar, Hans Urs. *The Grain of Wheat: Aphorisms*. San Francisco, CA: Ignatius Press, 1995.

_____. *Unless You Become Like This Child*. Erasmo Leiva-Merikakis trans. San Francisco, CA: Ignatius Press, 1991.

Watts, Alan. *Does it Matter? Essays on Man's Relation to Materiality*. New York: Vintage Books, 1971.

Weiss, Rick. "Free To Be Me: Would-Be Cloners Pushing the Debate." *The Washington Post*, May 12, 2002, pp A1 and A10.

Wertheimer, Margaret. *The Pearly Gates of Cyberspace: A History of Space from Dante to the Internet*. New York: W. W. Norton and Company, 1999.

Wiles, Maurice. "Christianity Without Incarnation?" In _The Myth of God Incarnate_. John Hick ed. Philadelphia, PA: The Westminster Press, 1977, pp. 1-10.

Woolley, Benjamin. _Virtual Worlds: A Journey in Hype and Hyperreality._ Oxford, UK and Cambridge, USA, 1992.

Young, Frances. "A Cloud of Witnesses." In _The Myth of God Incarnate_. John Hick ed. Philadelphia, PA: The Westminster Press, 1977, pp. 13-47.

Printed in the United States
18414LVS00001B/253-324